SPI
EGE
L&G
RAU

PRETTY IS
WHAT CHANGES

Impossible Choices, the Breast Cancer Gene,

and How I Defied My Destiny

Jessica Queller

SPIEGEL & GRAU

New York

2009

Published in the United States by Spiegel & Grau, an imprint of The Doubleday Publishing Group, a division of Random House, Inc., New York.
www.spiegelandgrau.com

A hardcover edition of this book was originally published in 2008
by Spiegel & Grau.
SPIEGEL & GRAU is a trademark of Random House, Inc.

BOOK DESIGN BY AMANDA DEWEY

Library of Congress Cataloging-in-Publication Data
Queller, Jessica, 1969–
Pretty is what changes : impossible choices, the breast cancer gene, and how I defied my destiny / Jessica Queller.
p. cm.
1. Queller, Jessica, 1969—Health. 2. Breast—Cancer—Patients—United States—Biography. 3. Breast—Cancer—Genetic aspects. I. Title.
RC280.B8Q48 2008
362.196'994490092—dc22
[B]
2008004303 s

ISBN 978-0-385-52041-6

PRINTED IN THE UNITED STATES OF AMERICA

For my mother

Pretty isn't beautiful, Mother,
Pretty is what changes.
What the eye arranges
Is what is beautiful.

—STEPHEN SONDHEIM,
"Sunday in the Park with George"

PRETTY IS
WHAT CHANGES

Glorious California light poured through the sunroof as I made the left turn, pulled up to the gate, smiled, and flashed my badge. Joe the security guard winked and bellowed, " 'Morning, Jess." The gate rose, and off I drove, the whole of the Warner Bros. lot spread before me. This routine never failed to give me a thrill.

When I was a little girl, my mother used to tell me I looked like Natalie Wood. At first I didn't know who she was, so my mom rented *Rebel Without a Cause* and *West Side Story* on Betamax and brought them home. Natalie Wood was so pretty—did my mother really think I looked like her? I watched the films over and over, straining to see a resemblance. My mother fixed this mythical and misguided ideal in my head: I was supposed to look like a starlet. I'd put on a white nightgown and sing "Tonight" into the mirror, assessing myself critically. Even at ten, I knew I fell short of Natalie Wood's beauty. But I certainly wasn't going to point this out to my mother.

My mother's projections were informed by the fact that she *did* look like a movie star. As a child, I'd curl up on the bathroom floor every morning and watch as she got ready for work. My mother would sit at her mirrored vanity table, carefully applying false eyelashes (a glamorous look from the 1960s that she continued well into the 1970s). She'd tell me how important it was for a woman to have a career, but, she added, a woman also had to be beautiful. "All girls are pretty when they're young," she'd say. "Once they grow up it's another story. Luckily you and your sister have my genes."

Now, more than twenty years later, I was working on the Warner Bros. lot where my beloved Natalie Wood had filmed *Rebel Without a Cause.* I acted blasé in front of my peers, but privately I found this astounding.

Though I'd wound up in Hollywood, I didn't work on the side of the camera my mother had destined for me—I was a writer on the hit television series *Gilmore Girls.* It took me a couple of decades to shed the notion that I was expected to measure up to movie stars. I'd finally achieved the balance and perspective to feel whole just as I was. But I'd never lose the capacity to be dazzled by Hollywood legends.

I drove past the steel suspension bridge, a perfect facsimile of an El train platform, where the doctors of *ER* bundled up against imagined Chicago cold, past the facade of a speakeasy covered in fake snow, and then I hit the jackpot: George Clooney and Don Cheadle playing a game of one-on-one at a netless hoop.

I made a right onto a street with a sign that read WELCOME TO WARNER VILLAGE. Neat rows of clapboard houses with emerald lawns and big shady trees lined each side of the street. To all appearances, it was a suburban neighborhood in New England. In reality, the exteriors of the houses were used for filming, while the interiors were divided into writers' offices. *Gilmore Girls* occupied two houses in the center of the lane.

I swung into my parking space and spotted some writers from another show indulging in the fantasy of our neighborhood by playing stickball up the street. As I cut the engine, my friend and fellow *Gilmore Girls* writer Rebecca sped into the parking space in front of mine. We stumbled out of our cars like upscale bag ladies—teetering on high heels, wearing dramatic sun hats and shades, weighted down with bags of scripts, notebooks, laptops. We saw our own crazy image reflected in the other and broke into laughter. Individually, we were able to maintain the semblance of being adult professionals; together, we regressed into a pair of mischievous twelve-year-olds playing dress-up.

Rebecca was twenty-nine, tall and striking with long, pale blond hair; she had the carriage and confidence of a young Kate Hepburn and a Harvard pedigree to back it up. I was thirty-four, brunette, more of the girl next door. There was no need to appear jaded to Rebecca. Our chemistry allowed us to be our most vulnerable, true selves. We also shared clothes and lipsticks and finished each other's sentences. Though we mocked ourselves for our excesses, we usually had far too much fun together to care.

"Did you get my message?" she asked.

"I've been trying to call you from the road. . . ."

"I've been trying to call *you* from the road. . . ."

"What did you say?" I asked.

"That I'm late and I need you to cover for me."

"You're not late," I said, glancing at the time on my cell phone. "It's nine thirty."

"I am late and so are you—we're gathering this morning at—"

"Nine! With Lorelai pitches. I forgot."

"I made up some pitches on the freeway while spilling my coffee and nearly crashing into one of those little VW Bugs with the stupid bud vase."

"Was there a bud in it?"

"A plastic rose." Rebecca started walking and I fell in beside her. "If you're going to buy a car with a built-in bud vase, you should at least make the effort to stick a live piece of greenery in it. This is California—pull something off a tree."

"Look," I said, pointing to our boss's parking space, "Amy's car's not here yet."

"Oh, good." She sighed. "I need to call the dog-walker. She took Nina to the vet."

"What's wrong with Nina?"

"She ate a box of doughnuts."

"Chocolate?"

"Assorted."

"What's the plan for tonight?"

"Eight thirty reservation at the Edendale."

"Perfect."

A softball rolled by our feet and one of the writers trotted over to retrieve it. He was a Harvard guy who'd been on the *Lampoon* with Rebecca. As they chatted, I walked up the porch steps and headed to my office.

The writers' PA, a boy of about twenty, greeted me with a bright hello and eagerly imparted the day's news: Our boss was running late and we wouldn't be gathering in the writers' room until ten. I thanked him for the update. He smiled shyly and I caught a sudden glimpse of myself through his eyes. To this kid who was paid next to nothing to answer the phones and make the coffee runs—all for the chance to be in proximity to those who were creating television—my life probably looked charmed. Of course it had only been a few years since I was scrambling to pay my rent and chasing a literary agent to his tennis lesson, imploring him to read my work. Now I breezed in every morning, a young woman with a high-powered, high-paying job writing for a popular TV show. But I was far more battle-worn than I appeared; I had recently experienced profound loss, and the interior of my life was not anywhere as neat as the facade. That said, there was no denying that I had been showered with great good fortune.

I tossed my bags on the sofa in my office, dropped into the desk chair, and checked my e-mail while going over a "to do" list scrawled on a lined yellow notepad. *Send rent check, buy shower gift for CM, call medical lab.* I wrote a check to my landlady while dialing the number for the lab.

"Westside Medical."

"Is this Mary?" I asked.

"Yes, it is."

"My name is Jessica Queller, I spoke to you yesterday. I'm trying to reach Dr. Williams."

"Regarding?"

"I took a blood test at your lab two months ago and I've been trying to obtain the results."

"What did you say your name was?"

"Jessica Queller. Q-u-e-l-l-e-r."

"Did you say you've called previously for the results?"

"Yes, Mary. I called yesterday, I called last week, I called the week before that."

"I found your file. That particular test is sent out to be performed by a different lab, miss. I'm afraid I don't know whether we've received the results yet."

"When I spoke to you yesterday, Mary, you said you were holding the envelope with my results in your hand. And you said that only the doctor was permitted to open it."

"I see. Would you hold, please?"

I cradled the receiver as cheesy music played through the phone. I hadn't bothered to meet the doctor when I went in for the test—a lab technician had taken my blood—so my name wouldn't hold any meaning for him. Still, I found it rude that he wasn't taking my calls. As one elevator song seeped into the next, I etched the yellow notepad with black ink, my frustration growing. Just as I was about to hang up and dial again, a man, his voice gruff and harried, came on the line.

"Who is this?"

"Jessica Queller. Are you Dr. Williams?"

"Yes."

"I've been trying to get you on the phone for weeks to obtain the results of a BRCA test I took in July."

"Who are you? Why did you take this test?"

I did not hide my irritation.

"My mother had breast cancer and died of ovarian cancer eleven months ago. My cousin, Dr. Alan Heilpern—your colleague—scheduled the appointment for me. I gave blood at your lab. I've left messages at your office repeatedly without the courtesy of a return phone call, and I can't understand why I've been unable to obtain the results."

"You tested positive for the BRCA-1 mutation," he said.

I tried to comprehend this statement. My immediate reaction was that the word *positive* sounded like a good thing, something positive. It took a few moments for my brain to process the fact that testing positive for a genetic mutation could not mean anything good.

"Positive is bad, right?"

"Right."

"How bad?"

"Statistically, you have up to an eighty-five or ninety percent chance of getting breast cancer."

I sat in shocked silence. It was as if this doctor were speaking in Swahili and expecting me to understand him. As if I'd fallen down the rabbit hole and decks of cards were talking. As if the logic and rules of my universe had suddenly changed. And in fact, they had.

The doctor's voice barked in my ear, "It's a very good thing you took this test."

Though I was reeling and couldn't grasp the meaning of the doctor's words, I knew instinctually that something momentous had occurred. I knew that his statement held some truth that would reveal itself in the months to come. And I knew on a gut level that this truth would change the course of my life.

ONE

November 2001

My mother declared that none of us were to leave the hospital until Harriette woke up. Her voice was tense, near frantic. She stood in the fluorescent-lit waiting room of Lenox Hill's ICU, her arms crossed. My sister and I sat on a sofa nearby. It was midnight. My grandmother Harriette Tarler had been a patient at Lenox Hill on and off for years, but recent kidney failure had landed her there permanently. Over the past few weeks she'd withered in fast-motion, like a movie playing at double-speed. She'd developed sepsis. This morning she'd fallen into a coma. The doctor did not expect her to wake up.

My mother looked out of place in this shabby waiting room—like a swan in a chicken coop. Her dark, luxurious hair evoked Jacqueline Bisset, though some people compared her to Diane Von Furstenberg. ("I'm much prettier than she is—her face is too broad," she'd insist.) My mother was five foot four but stood taller in her signature Manolo Blahnik stilettos. My mom had been wearing Manolos back when Sarah Jessica Parker was in diapers. In fact, my mother had been friends with Patricia Field—the costumer for *Sex and the City*—in the late seventies. As children, my sister Danielle and I spent hours sitting on the floor of Patricia Field's Eighth Street boutique, collecting pins and pushing them into a cotton tomato pincushion while our mom shopped. When I was about ten years old and Danielle six, Patricia asked our mom if Dani and I could appear in one of her fashion shows. We dressed up in sexy spandex and I disco-roller-skated alongside a dozen adult models while Danielle walked around the rink wearing her yellow rain boots because there were no roller skates in her small size. My mother had always been ahead of fashion trends, but in this instance she'd recognized the talent of Patricia Field twenty years before the rest of the world.

I had just arrived at the hospital after taking a flight from Los Angeles to New York, but my mother and Danielle had been there for eight hours without a break. My mother leaned against the arm of a vinyl reclining chair and said she was thirsty, so I went to the nurses' station to fetch her some water. When I returned, Dixie cup in hand, my mom was sitting next to my sister on the sofa. Though Danielle is tall and golden blond and our mother was petite and brunette, they were unmistakably mother and daughter. Danielle had inherited our mom's panache: an urban brand of beauty that turned men's heads and intimidated other women. Danielle had also adopted her style. They each wore layered cashmere and long, narrow pants of the same color—my mother all in black, my sister all in cream. The look was finished with a spectacular pair of heels and two or three pieces of expensive jewelry. My coloring and features resembled my mother's, but that's where the similarity ended. I'd been a struggling theater actress for years and had recently segued into writing. I was a "ragamuffin" (my mother's word) who clutched worn copies of Chekhov and made friends with homeless people on the street. During that time, to my mother's chagrin, my wardrobe consisted of sweaters with holes and old jeans. The closest thing to jewelry I owned was a string of thrift-store beads.

When our mother went to the ladies' room, Danielle briefed me on what I'd missed. On his rounds, Dr. Roth had informed them that Harriette's case was considered terminal, so she would not be allowed to remain in the ICU for long; the hospital needed the bed. He broached the subject of taking her off life support and our mom became hysterical. She insisted that Harriette would wake from her coma. "Harriette's threatened to die for ten years but she always bounces back," my mother cried. "Turning off the life support would be like murder! She *will* wake up." The doctor placed a compassionate hand on my mother's shoulder and promised to stall the bed issue as long as he could.

Dr. Roth was fond of Harriette—he'd been treating her for years and got a kick out of her. She'd given him glossy stills of herself as a young starlet with the Three Stooges. Harriette had been an aspiring actress in Hollywood in the 1950s. She'd had a recurring role as the French waitress in the Stooges pictures, which didn't prevent her from sometimes standing in as a girl who got a pie tossed in her face. In those days, her hair was a tawny shade of red and she dressed in form-fitting, slinky attire. Her nickname was "Tiger." When I was fourteen and won the coveted role of Abigail in the high school production of *The Crucible,* Harriette coached me on how to market myself as a professional actress: "It's not enough to be pretty and talented—you need a gimmick, a way to stand out. All the studio heads knew me as 'Tiger'—I'd sign my notes with a paw print." Long after she'd stopped acting and moved to New York, Harriette draped her apartment with tiger and leopard prints—the bedding, the rugs, the walls. As an old woman, she still resembled a tiger. She wore a floor-length fox-fur coat, colossal tortoiseshell glasses, and her hair long, silky, and golden red.

She also resembled a tigress in the ferocity with which she guarded her age. Danielle and I never called her Grandma when we were little, always Harriette. When Dani was around ten, she'd once made the mistake of addressing a letter from camp to "Grandma Harriette." This sparked an angry torrent: "I told you never to do that—now the doormen will guess how old I am!"

Our mother, too, had never called her Mom. When my mother turned sixteen, Harriette started taking her on weekends to Vegas, where they would double-date as sisters. By that time, Harriette had gone through three husbands—two divorces and one annulment. My mom's father had been Harriette's first, short-lived husband. He was a cruel man who remarried and forced my mother to babysit for his new children on the weekends of her court-ordered visits. He was also a deadbeat who contributed nothing to my mother's care and stole money her grandmother had willed to her. At sixteen, my mother cut him out of her life entirely and pretended he was dead.

When my mother was a senior in high school, Harriette moved into the Plaza Hotel in New York—the tab covered by one of her married boyfriends—leaving my mother to fend for herself, alone, in Los Angeles. My mother had a roof over her head, but no money. To get by, she babysat and often had meals at the neighbors'. For the rest of her life, my mother would be plagued by the fear that she would run out of money and end up destitute.

That night in the Lenox Hill waiting room, my mother did not allow for sleep. She was a drill sergeant, ordering me or Danielle to dart into the ICU every twenty minutes to check Harriette for signs of consciousness—a stirring, the flutter of an eyelid. Every so often, as if skeptical of our reports, she went in to check for herself. My mother was a willful creature—she'd worked as a fashion designer with her own label for over thirty years among aggressive, conniving men, some of them gangsters. "You have to be tough as nails to survive in the garment center," she often said with pride. As tough as she was, she had a damsel quality—an elusive aspect that made people want to take care of her. That night in the hospital, both sides were in evidence. She'd glance at her watch with a start: "It's been twenty-two minutes—Dani, Jessica, get in there!" She kept insisting that *when,* not *if,* Harriette woke up, one of us must be by her side. As the hours passed with no change, my mother grew panicked. Her bossiness could not hide her true emotional state, which was that of a terrified child. By four in the morning she was pacing, her eyes lit with fear. At fifty-eight, my mother had been spared any direct experience with death. Harriette had to be at least eighty (though she'd never admit it) and was riddled with illness, yet my mother was genuinely shocked to be told Harriette could actually *die.* I studied my mom, the intensity of her bewilderment. It struck me that this was not a usual display of grief. It struck me that until that night, my mother regarded death as a remote concept that affected other people. In her willful way, she was not prepared to allow death into her life.

Around seven in the morning, I escaped to the cafeteria on a coffee run. The line was long with residents in scrubs coming off the night shift, looking as bleary as I did. I sat down at a table, took out my cell phone, and dialed Kevin. It was the week before Thanksgiving. I was among thousands of American women who had flung themselves back into the arms of an ex-boyfriend on 9/11. Kevin and I hadn't talked in a couple of months, but the morning the towers fell he appeared on the doorstep of the Hollywood Hills guest house I rented and never left.

It was four a.m. in Los Angeles and I'd woken him from a dead sleep. I told him about Harriette's coma and my mother's frenzy, and he was sweet and supportive, as always, but I hung up feeling hollow. I'd stayed with Kevin for nearly two years though there had never been any real passion between us. A giant of a man, standing six foot five, Kevin also had an outsized heart. He was the guy who'd come over in the middle of the night to kill a bug. He would happily keep me company while I unpacked boxes or cleaned closets. Kevin was comforting, easy. Fondness and inertia had kept us together for so long. We cared for each other, but we were more like siblings than lovers. I'd only recently spurred myself to leave him, when tragedy tossed us right back into our warm but stagnant relationship. As I got on the cafeteria line, I resolved to end things with Kevin as soon as this ordeal was over.

Dr. Roth gave Harriette a reprieve in the ICU. Later that day, Danielle's new boyfriend, Bruce, dropped off a shipment of blankets and provisions, and we settled in for the second night of our vigil. People came and went, visiting other patients, surprised to see three grown women with fancy duvets camping out in a hospital waiting room.

That evening, a man was brought up to the ICU on a stretcher, and his wife and daughter joined us in what had by now become our lair. The man had been having a problem with his leg, and on their way to dinner he'd collapsed in the street. We watched the orderly wheel him into surgery—he was awake and rather cheerful. I chatted with the daughter, who, like me, was thirty-one. She was pretty and had a sharp sense of humor. We traded dating war stories. She told me that after a recent blind date, the guy demanded she reimburse him for half the price of dinner because she declined

to go out with him again. A few hours had passed when two doctors suddenly appeared, ushering mother and daughter into a private room. Their cries were piercing. I tried to fathom a woman
of my age facing the unexpected death of a parent. I couldn't.

Sometime the next day Danielle disappeared for an hour; when
she came back, her eyes were puffy and red. She'd been sitting
with Harriette and told me it finally hit her how dire things were
when she'd glanced at Harriette's hands. "Her manicure is a mess,"
Danielle said. "Harriette would never, under any circumstances,
have gone out in public without her nails perfectly groomed." Harriette had long, Streisand-esque talons, always painted in a neutral
French manicure. Danielle and my mother had the same hands,
down to the color of the polish. Nails that long were not the
fashion, but it was a timeless hallmark of the women in our family.
My own nails, however, were clipped and naked, with chewed-up
cuticles.

Around three in the morning of our third night at Lenox Hill,
my mother was dozing for the first time and my sister slept
soundly beside her. I slipped out of the waiting room and made
my way through the curtained sections of the ICU to Harriette's
bedside. Her skin looked translucent, like tissue paper. Her lips
were slightly parted and a pale shade of blue. I was overpowered
by a foul odor. It was a distinct rotting smell that I would never
forget.

I pulled up a metal chair and drew the curtain around us for
privacy. My thoughts ran through the details of her singular life.
In her later years, Harriette had become a sex therapist over the
phone, advertising in the back of *New York* magazine, using pseudo-
nyms like Cybil and Sharon, passing herself off as a woman in her
thirties and accepting payment from her clients by credit card.
She'd had a black Siamese cat named Tutankhamen who looked

like a miniature black panther. She toted him around Manhattan on a leash with a rhinestone collar that glittered like diamonds. Tut had an agent for print and television and was most famous for being the black cat in the Movado watch ads. When he died, she ordered a replica from the same breeder and named him Pharaoh. She grew exotic breeds of orchids on the terrace of her Manhattan apartment. Harriette was more colorful than a kaleidoscope—the last thing anyone expected from a grandmother—and Danielle adored her, idolized her. Everyone was charmed by her. Everyone but me.

I had been harboring anger toward Harriette for as long as I could remember. When I acted in my first professional play at fifteen, people said, "Oh, you take after your grandmother," and I haughtily replied that I took after my father, a renowned trial lawyer who had great stage presence. The source of my anger had to do with my mother. My mom had hurt my feelings, disappointed me repeatedly over the years, yet I'd never uttered a word and had rarely blamed her. All the blame was saved for Harriette.

Though affectionate and well-meaning, my mother lacked basic mothering skills. Harriette had been as maternal as Medea, so my mother was left to pick up clues from other sources, like TV shows. From June Cleaver she gleaned what a family should look like. Though she always worked, my mom cooked and cleaned on the weekends; she kept the household looking pretty and orderly. She roasted a big turkey at Thanksgiving and bought pumpkins for us at Halloween, because those were the sort of things she thought normal families did. My mother's attention was fixed on exteriors. When I was in high school, she'd devote two hours to setting my thick hair in hot rollers for an audition, yet she would not know the names of my teachers or friends, never mind the name of the play I was trying out for. She was the only Jewish mother I knew who took no interest in her daughter's love life. In my early twenties it was a year before she learned my boyfriend's last name, though she would dedicate weeks to hunting in flea markets for just the right piece of furniture for my apartment. That was her way of giving—through the material.

From a young age I understood that she was a far superior mom to what *she* had as a mother. Granted, my father—the only other person immune to Harriette's charms—fed me these ideas, but I knew them to be true. (At the time of Harriette's coma my parents had recently divorced—however, my dad would never have sat vigil for Harriette, even if they'd still been married; he disliked her for the way she treated my mother.) When I got the highest possible score on two Advanced Placement exams in the twelfth grade, my mom replied, "That's nice," and I watched the information evaporate around her head like steam. Her voice, though, was full of warmth when she steered the conversation to the pair of Joan and David leather boots she'd bought for me—she'd spotted them in the window and thought they looked old-fashioned and were just my style. My mother was sweet in her way, and doing her best, whereas Harriette was unabashedly competitive and out for herself.

I gazed at my frail, decaying grandmother, asleep in her coma, her prized nails now chipped and gray. I'd been giving a lot of thought to the fact that I didn't want Harriette to die while I remained so full of resentment. I pulled *The Tibetan Book of Living and Dying* out of my bag. I had a casual interest in Buddhism and I'd come across a chapter in this book that had sparked an idea: I read about a form of meditation called Tonglen—a kind of prayer to be done for a person while she's dying—and I thought practicing it at Harriette's bedside might possibly help me. At the same time, I cringed at how flaky and new-agey this experiment would appear, so I'd waited for a moment of privacy. The author translated *Tonglen* as "active compassion." I closed my eyes and followed the instruction, contemplating all the pain Harriette had suffered near the end of her life. To my amazement, it worked. My heart unclenched, tears flowed. I was overcome with emotion. I realized that throughout my years of condemning her, it had never once occurred to me to wonder what *Harriette's* mother had been like. I felt deep grief for her. I felt grateful that my mother was still in her prime. I felt thankful for my own life. At thirty-one, I was finally beyond the painful struggle for identity that had plagued my twenties. I was coming into my own. I had a flash of gratitude for the joy I felt certain was right around the corner.

THAT MORNING, November 18, 2001, Harriette died without fanfare. Her breathing grew labored; a nurse called us in. "It's time," she said. My mother, sister, and I stood around Harriette, holding her hands and stroking her hair as she made her exit.

TWO

December 2001

Throughout our Lenox Hill hospital stay, my mother had regularly complained of stomach pain. Danielle and I had assured her this was perfectly normal. Her mother was dying—who wouldn't have a stomachache?

Exactly two weeks after Harriette's death, we were back in the hospital. This time it was the NYU emergency room and the patient was my mother. Her stomach was the size of a large melon and the pain had grown so severe she couldn't stand. She was suffering from nausea and vomiting. We soon learned that her stomach distention was due to ascites—abdominal fluid that accumulates as a response to advanced cancer.

A few days later, my mother underwent emergency laparoscopic surgery. Another waiting room. This time my sister and I were joined by our father. Everything was a blur.

We were told that my mother had stage IIIC ovarian cancer. We knew this wasn't good news, but aside from that, we didn't know exactly what it meant. At age fifty-two, my mother had successfully beaten stage II breast cancer. Would this be a harder fight? When my mother was out of recovery, the surgeon stopped by her hospital room and informed us he was able to remove most of the cancer, but not all of it, because it was strewn around her stomach like small "grains of rice." My mother held on to this image. In the months to come she would tell everyone she was all better except for "a few scattered grains of rice."

Years later I would order her hospital records. The summary of this single operation was four pages long. What it makes clear is that the cancer was everywhere.

The hospital stay lasted sixteen days. Danielle and I never left our mother's side. We shared a small cot and slept beside her every night.

Several days post-op, my mother was sitting up in bed, alert, taking stock of her situation. A dark-haired woman, a doctor, stopped by the room holding a medical chart. I can remember her face, her voice, but I now have no idea who she was. My mother drilled her with questions. In response to one, the woman replied, "We still consider your condition curative."

Still?

My mother jumped all over this. "How many years can I be expected to live?"

The woman hesitated. "About five years," she replied.

She exited, leaving me, my mother, and Danielle in stunned silence. *Five years to live?* It was worse than anything we could have imagined.

In fact, she would live less than two.

A FEW WEEKS LATER, still walking around in a daze, I met a woman named Leslie Rosen for coffee, at the insistence of my friend Gillian. Leslie had started a foundation for the prevention of women's cancer, in honor of her mother, who had died of ovarian cancer a couple of years earlier. She was a font of information on the subject, and Gillian felt it would be helpful for me to talk to her.

Leslie was around my age, and as it happened, the oncologist who was treating my mother had also treated hers.

"He's the best doctor in the country," she said.

I wondered how she could speak of the doctor's talent with such conviction when her mother, his patient, had died.

She asked me a few questions, and I revealed that my mother had suffered from, and beaten, breast cancer six years earlier. Leslie told me that the women's clinic she'd founded offered a cutting-edge genetic test for a mutation that predisposed women to breast and ovarian cancer. That was the first time I'd heard those two cancers linked.

"Because of your mother's history, you're now in the highest-risk category. You're the perfect candidate for this genetic test."

She described the test at length, encouraging me to consider it and to talk to a genetic counselor. Leslie was in the same high-risk category, so I asked if she'd taken it. She lowered her eyes and said no. "Why not?" I asked. She said she wanted to enjoy her marriage and finish having kids before accepting the burden of that kind of knowledge.

At the time, I didn't grasp what Leslie meant about the burden of knowledge. I remember thinking it was odd that she had founded a cancer prevention clinic that boasted an exclusive genetic test for high-risk women, and yet she had not taken the test herself.

I doubted my mother's cancer was genetic since Harriette had never had cancer, nor had Harriette's sister or mother. Still, I thought it would be prudent for me to find out for sure, at some point, by taking the test. I was consumed with my mother's illness; my own health was not a present concern. I had just turned thirty-two. If I turned out to be at high risk, I believed it was something I'd have to worry about when I was around fifty. I stored the knowledge of this gene test away, and did not think of it again for two and a half years.

THREE

My father was born at Dr. Leff's Hospital in the Bronx. Was there really a hospital called Dr. Leff's? "Of course there was," my dad said. "It's gone now—they arrested Dr. Leff for performing illegal abortions."

My dad grew up in a one-bedroom tenement apartment on East 116th Street in Spanish Harlem with his parents, Victor and Helen, and his brother, Leon. He slept on a dingy sofa in the foyer until the age of twenty, and spent those first twenty years working in his parents' mom-and-pop hardware store on East 112th Street. When my dad was six, his mother brought him to P.S. 101 to start the first grade. The teacher went down the list of names, and when she called out "Fred Queller?" Helen nudged my dad forward. The teacher welcomed him and gave him some instructions. My dad turned to his mother, bewildered, and said in Yiddish, *"Vos zugt ze?"* ("What is she saying?") He did not understand a word of English.

But my father was a quick study. A few years later he went to a yeshiva in the Bronx where he became an honors student. He was accepted to Stuyvesant—the best public high school in Manhattan—where he was elected senior class president. Then he went to City College. He finally moved out of the house (and slept in a real bed for the first time) when he attended NYU Law School on scholarship. He made *Law Review* and completed NYU in two and a half years. He went to work as a lawyer for a solo practitioner who paid him a mere forty dollars a week but allowed him to bring in his own cases and put his name on the door. Soon my dad had his own bachelor pad in Washington Square Village in the new art deco high-rises on Bleecker Street. He drove a Cadillac convertible and was known as "the Dancing Lawyer."

"I never learned how to play ball as a kid because I was too busy working in the store. But I was strong from physical labor—I was the delivery boy, lugging boxes of linoleum on my back to our customers. In high school, when everybody else played ball, I worked out on the ropes, the horse, the mats. And I liked girls, so I went to the Young Men's Hebrew Association on Sunday afternoons and learned how to dance. In those days it was the fox-trot, the rhumba, the mambo, the samba, the cha-cha. I became very good—you know me when I set my mind to something. That's how I became known as 'the Dancing Lawyer.'"

By 1965 "the Dancing Lawyer" knew "Harriette the Actress" from the singles scene in New York. One summer night at a Fourth of July party, Harriette showed up with a beautiful young woman. Fred samba-ed over.

"Harriette, who's that girl you're with?"

"That's my kid sister, Stephanie. She's visiting from California." Soon enough, Stephanie, the burgeoning fashion designer, moved into Fred's bachelor pad. They were married, and Harriette was outed as the mother.

Fred had moved into Washington Square Village at the age of twenty and would live in those buildings until he was seventy-one. My parents upgraded to a two-bedroom in 1969 when I was born, then moved to a three-bedroom on the thirteenth floor when Danielle was born in 1973. Ten years later they rented the one-bedroom apartment next door and broke the wall down to create a lavish Greenwich Village spread. Fred was the original tenant in the building, and the apartments were rent-controlled. When he moved out in 2004, the rent for his five-bedroom/two-living-room place was lower than the market value of a studio apartment.

My parents were self-made dynamos in their respective careers. They typically came home from work after Danielle and I had already been put to bed by the housekeeper. To make up for this, they devoted weekends to us children.

As a designer my mother helped forge fashion trends, and through the years the decor of our apartment reflected the style of the times. In the early seventies the walls were painted brown and the carpeting was orange, the furniture Spanish, dark wood. In the late seventies/early eighties everything was beige—the walls, sofas, tapestries, rugs. In the mideighties, my father got his turn to decorate and created a formica-and-mirror palace. A large, gray modern sculpture stood in the foyer and two Erté drawings hung in the living room, framed in gold. Though the eighties modern fad was outdated almost the moment it arrived, my parents had spent so much money on the custom-made furniture that filled every room they never again redecorated. This decor stretched on into the nineties and began to fall apart—formica curling up at the corners and vertical blinds falling like dead leaves. When Danielle left for college, she bought our dad a black Lab puppy named Samson as a present. Sam ruled the roost, slobbering on the faded gray leather sofas, chewing on the legs of chairs, further turning the apartment into a madhouse. It was in this setting, in December of 1994, that my father casually asked my mother one night over a take-out Japanese dinner if she'd gotten the results back from her routine mammogram.

"Yes," she answered, chopsticks balancing a piece of sushi. "Apparently there was a barely discernible spot on the film, but my doctors say they think it's fine."

My dad was now a famous trial lawyer and a dynamo of a medical malpractice attorney. He pounced.

"What do you mean they *think* it's fine?"

The next day my father escorted my mother to the office of the esteemed breast surgeon Dr. Daniel Roses, who performed a needle biopsy. The barely discernible spot turned out to be cancer that had already spread to five lymph nodes. My mother had an immediate lumpectomy, after which she underwent four cycles of Adriamycin followed by Cytoxan—aggressive chemotherapies. Then she underwent radiation. She had just turned fifty-two.

In the months before my mother's diagnosis of breast cancer, I was angry at her.

Reaching the age of fifty (two years earlier) had left my mother blinking in disbelief. She was a beauty who turned heads when she entered a room. Just like Harriette before her, my mother felt fifty was the beginning of life's inevitable decline. It sent her into a tailspin. She refocused on her own life with a vengeance—doubling her time on the StairMaster, pouring herself into her business. From my point of view, she'd become shrouded in a fog of narcissism, unable to see beyond herself.

Our birthdays were one day apart in November; as my mother turned fifty-two, I turned twenty-five. I was in pain over my career as an actress—a career that was alive only with the faintest pulse. I'd been dumped by the agency that had represented me since I was fifteen, signed by another, and was on the verge of being dumped again. My close friends were starring on Broadway in Tennessee Williams and Arthur Miller revivals, while my prospects were diminishing. My struggles were deeper, though, than just being unemployed. I had begun to lose confidence in myself, in my judgment. I'd been acting in plays since I was a child and had always believed theater was the right medium for my talents and creativity. Evidence had been accumulating that I was wrong. I felt lost, in crisis, ashamed. It was a typical affliction of people in their twenties, but that knowledge didn't ease my suffering.

My mother had always been oblivious to the details of my life, but she was usually warm and loving. Now something had turned. She seemed barely aware of my presence, and when she did take me in, she was cold. I'd been away for a month trying to hustle work in Los Angeles and stopped by my parents' apartment the night I got back. My mother wandered into the living room, where I was talking to my father, and said blankly, "Oh, I didn't know you were here," and walked out of the room. She'd always had hang-ups about money and they were flaring up. It irritated her that my father was helping me financially. The lavish birthday party he'd thrown for her at the Rainbow Room and the yellow diamond ring the size of a house he'd bought her did not appease her. I was hurt and angry, and for the first time I did not deflect the blame to Harriette. Right before she was diagnosed with breast cancer, I was—after years of swallowing my feelings—on the verge of lashing out.

I'd started quietly rebelling against my mother's values years earlier. When I left for college in 1987, I was uncomfortable in my own skin, embarrassed by the person I'd been raised to be. To compensate, I performed self-loathing comic monologues about being a Jewish American Princess from Manhattan for my freshman roommate, Kay. Tears of laughter rolled down her cheeks as I described my humiliation in the sixth grade over showing up at my hip Greenwich Village school in the dead of winter with a dark tan, which tipped the other kids off to the fact that my parents had a condo in Boca. Away from my family, I set about the task of trying to re-create myself. The only signpost I had was my desire to differentiate myself from my mother. She was a fashion designer; I yearned to be an intellectual. She wore Armani, Chanel, Prada; I wore sacklike thrift-store dresses. She dressed in clothes to flaunt her figure; I bought everything oversized to hide my curves. I was drawn to women friends who possessed qualities I wanted to emulate, qualities my mother lacked. Kay, my best friend, was a fiercely intelligent, no-nonsense wry wit who had spent her unhappy childhood in Mississippi reading everything under the sun. I became a literature major, though I continued to act in plays as I had in high school. Of course I couldn't see at the time that being an actress, even one doing Ibsen and Shakespeare, had obvious elements in common with my mother—the narcissism, the emphasis on beauty and on being admired.

As a little girl I looked so much like my mother that she called me her "clone." She named me Tiffany after *Breakfast at Tiffany's,* the movie starring Audrey Hepburn. Her name was Stephanie and my name was Tiffany, and she reveled in telling everyone we were exactly alike. Cringing over the name Tiffany began for me early in grade school. I went to a Quaker school on East Sixteenth Street with the children of Greenwich Village's avant-garde artists—Phillip Glass and Lee Brewer among them. The other kids had names like Clove and freely roamed the streets of New York by age ten. My father was overprotective and didn't want his girls taking the public bus, so he hired a driver to take me and Danielle to school. I was mortified. I insisted on being dropped off a block away, but this didn't trick anyone. In the seventh grade, a black girl in my class told me, not unkindly, that my father's chauffeur played jazz at night with her father. I wanted to die. All my feelings of shame became wrapped up in the name Tiffany. I could change schools, take the subway, change clothes, but I could not escape the stigma of my powder-puff name. By college, the name was my albatross. It depressed me, caused me severe self-consciousness. I believed my name defeated me from the start—boxing me into a category of shallow, frivolous women.

At twenty-one, I decided to change it legally. I had enough sense to know that to go from Tiffany to something exotic like Maya or India would be ridiculous. I wanted a simple, pleasant name that could adapt to who *I* was. Unfortunately, I didn't have a middle name to use, so I chose something quickly and arbitrarily. I went to see a friend play Jessica in a production of *The Merchant of Venice* and decided that would do. Changing my name from Tiffany was an explicit rejection of my mother, and I agonized over telling her. When I finally did, she looked at me with big eyes and said in a singsongy voice, "That's so funny. I was just thinking the other day that I didn't like the name anymore and I wondered if it bothered you." I stared back in bewilderment. My father filed the legal papers. No one has called me anything but Jessica since.

Four years later, I was twenty-five and fuming. Shortly after my mother had snubbed me in her living room, I was gearing up to unleash a lifetime of pent-up hurt and feelings of abandonment. Before I had the chance, my mother was diagnosed with breast cancer. The tension that had been building between us evaporated.

My mother was sick—all else was moot. That said, my mother, sister, and I did not grasp the gravity of breast cancer. The possibility of death was never considered. We understood she had an illness, and that was rattling enough to our sheltered family. However, my father knew what breast cancer was. When they were given the news in the doctor's office, he started to cry. My mother was taken aback, as my father rarely showed emotion.

My mother was shocked to be diagnosed with cancer. She didn't smoke or drink, she was a careful eater, she was slim, she was a runner. How could this have happened to her?

What breast cancer meant to my mother was losing her hair. To any woman this would be a terrible blow, but to my mother it was pure horror. The night of her lumpectomy, I lay in a cot next to her hospital bed while *Roman Holiday* played in the background. We had turned on the TV for some distraction, but my mother's gaze was fixed and vacant. She reflexively stroked her pretty, dark mane over and over. Only worse than losing her hair, she said, would be to lose her breasts. "Thank God," she kept repeating like a mantra. What she meant was thank God she had the kind of cancer that allowed for a lumpectomy. The way she understood it, the cancer had already spread to her lymph nodes, so there was no need to have a mastectomy. I would find out years later that she'd gotten it wrong: It was not the lymph node involvement that made her eligible for lumpectomy, it was that her tumor had clear margins. But to her mind, a little more advanced cancer was far preferable to losing her breasts.

Once out of the hospital from breast surgery, my mother flew into action. She found the most exclusive wig-maker in New York and promptly ordered four wigs made to look exactly like her hair. She instructed the wig-maker how to make a concoction of her own design: sewing bangs into the front of a Yankees cap and attaching a long brown ponytail to the back. This would be worn during her six-mile weekend runs in the Hamptons. She ordered two of them. Regardless of nausea, vomiting, mouth sores, or lymphedema, my mother exercised on the StairMaster every weekday morning, got dressed in her Armani suits and Manolos, caught the subway, and was in her designer showroom by nine. When her hair started falling out in clumps, she put on the custom-made wigs. She never missed a day of work, scheduling chemo appointments during her lunch hour, and wowed nurses and patients with her spike heels and movie-star clothes. She didn't tell anyone outside of our immediate family about her breast cancer. Gradually, people at work noticed her sallow complexion, her swollen arm, that her hair was a wig. When asked how she was, she stuck to her story: She was fine and well. My mother brazenly refused to be sick, and she was not going to enable anyone else to view her that way.

The months passed. She finished her treatments, her hair grew back, and she *was* well. She had triumphed over breast cancer. For a few weeks she talked to me about helping her write a book about beauty for cancer patients: "There's absolutely nothing out there for the modern woman about how to stay beautiful while on chemo, and I've figured it all out!" But the idea fell quickly by the wayside. She was eager to resume her normal life and leave illness behind. And she did just that. She lived every day to the fullest for six years, until the age of fifty-eight, when she was struck again—this time with ovarian cancer.

JANUARY 2002. We checked in at the front desk.

"My name is Stephanie Queller, I'm here for chemo."

Perhaps it was the difficult recovery from abdominal surgery or perhaps it was because she'd traded in her heels for shiny black

Chanel ballerina flats, but my mother appeared much smaller than before.

The nurse practitioner, Andrea, a pretty woman with ginger-colored hair, warmly welcomed my mother, said she'd been expecting her. The effect was Julie the cruise director welcoming her to purgatory. Danielle and I were like my mother's wings—we hovered on either side of her and went wherever she went. I hadn't returned to Los Angeles after Harriette's death. My friends helped sublet my guest house and, though I'd recently launched a new career as a TV writer, I told my agent I needed to remain in New York for a while. Not returning to California presented a natural opening for me to end things with Kevin.

Andrea led the three of us into a back room where she drew my mother's blood. This would become a ritual: Every session before receiving chemo my mother would give blood for a CA-125 test. It remains the best existing tool for monitoring the disease status in patients known to have ovarian cancer. The results are given in numbers—the lower the number, the better. If she got a higher number than she did a few weeks earlier, the chances were the chemo wasn't working and her cancer was spreading. The day after chemo was always a sickening experience of waiting for the numbers, like a perverse lottery game in which the prize was my mother's life.

Next, Andrea led my mother to a large reclining armchair and hooked her up to an IV pole that fed clear liquid chemotherapy into her veins. The room was long and narrow with a wall of windows facing the East River. Each chemo recliner had its own little section by the window, with a couple of chairs for guests. Turkey and tuna sandwiches on white bread and boxes of juice were available for patients in a minirefrigerator. There was a hush in the room, like you would find in a library. It was pleasant to look out at the water and watch the barges go by.

After the initial shock of my mother's prognosis subsided, we went about the business at hand—resolving to beat the cancer. My mother was extremely competitive. She believed she could do what no one else could do. "I'll show them," she'd said defiantly to me and Danielle the first night she'd been well enough to have dinner out at a restaurant. "If they say I have five years to live, I'll live ten." We all agreed over dim sum that if anyone could beat the odds, she could—and that ten years from now there would probably be a cure for cancer.

My mother, Danielle, and I settled into our nook overlooking the river. My mother opened a glossy magazine, her customized MedicAlert bracelet—crafted out of chunky gold links and diamond studs—dangling from her wrist. She'd designed it herself: "If you have to wear something for medical purposes, why shouldn't it be a beautiful piece of jewelry?" Danielle went to get us sandwiches; I glanced around the floor. As usual, the chemo chairs were full. The patients spanned from young to old, in different stages of hair loss. Many wore wigs. My mother's brown hair was conspicuously graying at the roots. Knowing she had to start chemo, she had decided to stop stressing her hair with dye. She was resolved to do whatever it took to defeat cancer with one caveat: She refused to lose her hair. She insisted that her oncologist treat her only with drugs that did not induce hair loss. Losing her hair was the one indignity she could not bear to repeat.

Danielle returned from the kitchen area and handed us turkey sandwiches. I watched my mom nibble at the bread and page through *Vogue* while toxic chemicals dripped into her veins. My mother's usual luster was absent. She still had plenty of fight in her, but we all knew that, this time, things were different.

FOUR

June 2002

Something wonderful happened. I got a writing job on a hit television series that filmed in New York. In the past year I'd established myself as a writer of one-hour "dramedies"—funny, character-based shows about relationships. There were only a handful of dramedies on-air, which meant the window for employment was tiny. This series was the only one of its kind filming in New York that year. The single, highly coveted job in my field that would enable me to both move forward in my career and be near my sick mother had just dropped from the sky. What were the chances?

There was one small glitch. Nine years earlier, at twenty-three, I had gotten into a vicious fight with a girl over my then-boyfriend. Jonathan Marc Sherman is a playwright, and our four-year relationship was full of drama. Throughout the years, we would famously break up for a week or so and then get back together. This girl, who had become entangled with him during one of our off-weeks, wanted to hang around once I was back in the picture, and I was not having it. It was a clash of notable intensity, and she and I had not seen each other since. She'd grown up to become a successful actress and, as fate would have it, she was the star of this show. I decided to call Lisa to clear the air before work began. I expected to laugh off the behavior of our younger selves, schedule a date for coffee, and become friends. Granted, my call caught her off-guard, but it did not go well. She was tense and abrupt. I hung up feeling uneasy.

I had found the perfect New York sublet—a small but charming one-bedroom walk-up on Barrow Street in the West Village. The restaurant One if by Land, Two if by Sea, a romantic landmark set in an old carriage house, was my next-door neighbor. My rickety building was set back in a courtyard and had full advantage of the lush gardens that ringed the restaurant. In the stairwell, the paint was peeling and the carpet threadbare, but decent prints hung in old frames on the walls and the overall vibe was artsy. The apartment itself had wood-beamed ceilings and a working fireplace. It was a gem.

I was grateful to be employed in New York so I could be close to my mother, but I had not anticipated just how close. Shortly after beating breast cancer, my mother had quit the garment center. She felt that the stress of her career might have contributed to her getting cancer, so she walked away from designing clothes after thirty-seven years and resolved to create a more peaceful life. Within a year, she'd opened a store of antique dishes and glassware in Southampton that rivaled the top floor of Bergdorf's. It was a serious business that required a lot of work, but at least the setting was the bucolic Hamptons.

Part two of her life change was walking away from her thirty-five-year marriage. In a rather late midlife crisis, my mother di-

vorced my father, claiming she'd married too young and never had
the chance to find herself—she'd gone straight from a rocky life
with Harriette to living with Fred. They had separated two years
before her ovarian cancer diagnosis, and during that time she'd
lived on Long Island full-time. Suddenly, she needed to be in the
city several days a week for doctors' appointments. After Harriette died, my mother began renovating her Midtown apartment;
it was still under construction, which meant my mother had no
place to stay. That's how she wound up moving into the Barrow
Street apartment with me.

There was one queen-size bed, and my mother and I shared it
three, sometimes four or five nights a week. I never knew how
to answer the question "Are you close to your mother?" We'd
gone through that strained period when I was twenty-five that
fizzled out when she got sick. Overall, we didn't speak the same
language, and she didn't follow the saga of my daily life, but we
had a primal closeness. I was prone to nightmares and even as
a grown-up I would sometimes call and wake my mom in the
middle of the night to be assured that it was just a bad dream and
all was well. People thought it was extreme that my sister and I
spent every night with my mother in the hospital, sleeping on a
cot. They called that kind of closeness "unusual." It never occurred
to us that it could be otherwise—it was a given in our family that
my mother would never be left alone. Similarly, when my mother
needed a place to stay, though I was a thirty-two-year-old working
woman, there was never any question that she could crash with
me and share my bed.

During the day, my mother was a dynamo—always moving,
shopping, working. No one would guess she was a cancer patient
on aggressive chemotherapy. The hours of my new job were gruel-
ing—I'd leave at nine in the morning and get home around one or

two a.m. During the seven or eight hours spent in the apartment, I was desperate for sleep, but would get very little. At night, my mother was haunted by her cancer. Propped up on the pillows in a silk nightie, she would voice her fears. "What if the little grains of rice are spreading? What if the chemo isn't working? What if my CA-125 numbers go up? What will become of me?" She was terrified that she might have only five years to live. "There are so many things I've always wanted to do—now my time is running out. Where do I begin?" She sat up all night, every night, eyes wide with fear. I was just as scared, but I tried my best to console her. Sometimes she cried; the rest of the time she stared into the darkness. She never slept.

Then there was the new job. The writers began work several weeks before the actors so that scripts could be written and ready for production. The show was going into its third season, and with two exceptions the writing staff from the previous year had been fired and we were all brand-new. The creators of the show sequestered themselves in a private wing of the production offices, never to be seen. They communicated with the writing staff via messages delivered by a minion who scurried back and forth between their offices and the writers' room. The new head writer, or "show-runner," Adrian—my immediate boss—was baffled by this system. He was a former stand-up comic with an extremely dry, twisted sense of humor. He was low-key, generous to writers, and his understated, ironic way of speaking was pitch-perfect. We all loved him.

Writers shared personal stories in the room, and the result was we got to know one another fast. Adrian was a dark character. His first wife, Cinnamon, had been an exotic dancer. They had a child together. Bill Maher was a friend of Adrian's and had once told him, "You don't *marry* the girl who jumps out of the cake."

Once, Cinnamon sued Adrian on *The People's Court* for throwing a car seat at her, bruising her leg and causing her to miss work. Adrian's defense to Judge Wapner was one terse, ironic line: "Your Honor, she's a *stripper*." He lost. He was fined two hundred dollars. When things didn't work out with Cinnamon, Adrian found a new, lovely wife while he was abroad doing a comedy tour and brought her back to the States to raise his kid. They had three more children. He'd recently left her and she was reportedly heartbroken. Adrian was charming and warm in the writers' room, but he had a chilling lack of empathy. No topic was too sacred for his scathing humor: his divorce, terrorist attacks, suicide. It was once said of Charles Bukowski: "He was a very tender-hearted guy—not towards people necessarily, but towards goldfish." When I read that quote years later, I thought of Adrian.

On day four of the job, we'd left the writers' room for a five-minute break and had scattered to our respective offices when, suddenly, an e-mail from Adrian appeared on my screen. It read: "Hey. How's work?" I was surprised and flustered. From another type of guy, perhaps this could be construed as an innocent inquiry—not from this man. I understood the meaning and implication of that three-word e-mail at once. It was the Hugh Grant moment in the first *Bridget Jones*. Though not as florid as "You appear to have forgotten your skirt," it was the moment of crossing a boundary, establishing private dialogue, initiating flirtation. I remember staring at the screen, feeling flushed, aware of imminent danger. This guy was incredibly attractive. Handsome, seductive, with ice-blue eyes and a knowing glint. Though he was separated from his second wife, she still called the office several times a day. On top of which he was my *boss*. My computer screen might as well have been flashing *BEWARE* in fiery letters. My first instinct was that I must not engage. Could I just ignore the e-mail? Then

I told myself I was overreacting. He was flirting, so what? I could handle myself. I dashed off an equally innocuous response to his note ("Work's great"), shut down the computer, and returned to the writers' room as if nothing had happened. That was the beginning of my descent.

THE FIRST FEW DAYS following her chemo treatment, my mother would become extremely nauseous. Those nights and mornings would be spent on the cold tiles of Barrow Street's tiny bathroom floor. I held my mom's hair back while she hung over the toilet, trying to decide whether she was finished or was going to be seized by another bout of sickness. My mom had cut her hair to just above the shoulders, which, for her, was short. Because she'd been growing out the color, the top half of her hair was now silvery gray, while the bottom half remained brown. It was a strange, two-toned look, but she preferred it to cutting her hair any shorter. For the first time in over twenty years, my mother stopped exercising. She told me that walking required all of her strength.

WITHIN TWENTY-FOUR HOURS of the Hugh Grant move, Adrian was giving me the full-court press. Nobody knew, of course. The first eight weeks of the job were about Resisting Adrian and required monumental effort. It became rapidly clear that he had no moral compass. I called him Mephistopheles, which he loved. Like the devil, he was intelligent and achingly seductive, a sensualist, with persuasive arguments for joining him on the dark side. I had always been a good girl—the most rebellious thing I'd ever done was legally change my name. Even if he had been a person of decent character, this job was the one positive thing in my life—getting involved with my boss would jeopardize not only my job, but my reputation in the industry, too. To protests that he was my boss, Adrian replied: "So what? This is the stuff legends are made of. Our love cannot be hidden." Adrian bandied the word *love* about like a badminton birdie. He claimed he'd fallen in love with me at first sight. Many of the things he said sound ridiculous on paper—it was his half-earnest, half-ironic, twinkle-eyed delivery that would slay me. The pull toward him was magnetic. He'd stop by my desk under the pretense of some work matter, catch my eyes with his hypnotic gaze, and try to persuade me to go on a date with him. I'd fall deeply under his spell for a minute or two and then snap myself out of it with a jolt. Rattled, I'd ask him to please refrain from ruining my life as I proceeded to throw him (my boss) out of my office.

Even in the earliest stages, I saw Resisting Adrian as a kind of epic battle, with my soul in the balance. I had worked hard at becoming the woman of integrity I wanted to be—one slip and I could wipe out years of effort. Was I really going to throw myself away over this indulgence? I was afraid I might. When I was apart from him, I was clear. But in his presence my mind melted, and I was being paid to sit in a writers' room with him for twelve hours a day. I resorted to creative antics to stop myself from yielding: I hand-copied passages from books that had moral weight and taped them around the apartment, hoping they'd serve as an antidote. I put up quotes from Joseph Campbell, Buddhist texts, and the twelve steps of Alcoholics Anonymous. While I was arming myself with wisdom of the ages, the actors finally arrived. What happened next was so uncanny it seemed scripted. The actress Lisa met Adrian just once and began an immediate, aggressive pursuit of *him,* unwittingly re-creating our romantic triangle. While I was summoning moral fortitude to resist his advances, the beautiful blond starlet—my former rival—was parading around the writers' offices, flouncing into Adrian's desk chair.

Lisa was everything I was not, which is what had made her threatening to me the first time around. We were a variation on Betty and Veronica. She was the all-American blond cover girl who had effortlessly ascended as a star in TV and film. I was a brunette writer and failed actress who self-destructed in front of the camera. My inability to get a headshot photo in which I wasn't grimacing was one of the factors that had led me to quit. She was athletic and outdoorsy. At the time she'd just filmed some cable special in which she swam with dolphins. I was a Woody Allen–style neurotic New Yorker who stayed out of direct sunlight. In spite of the Alice-in-Wonderland looks that landed Lisa ingenue parts, offscreen her sexuality was bold and explicit. In the table-reading for the first episode of the show, she wore a black T-shirt with two fried eggs where her breasts would be. I was her negative image in my feminine white peasant blouses. The office was abuzz with the flirtation of Adrian and the actress. By this point, Adrian knew of my history with Lisa and tried to use it as ammunition: "I won't go out with her if you'll agree to see me." I rolled my eyes and stood my ground. They went on a date. I was in pain. I was curious to note how acute the pain was. I tried to detach from it, observe it as a sociological study. Beneath the pain, however, I believed this turn of events to be good luck. Getting involved with Adrian would be a certain train wreck. The best thing that could happen to me and my higher self would be for Adrian to become Lisa's boyfriend.

About a week passed, during which Adrian was constantly getting buzzed on the intercom in the writers' room and told that Lisa was on the phone. I couldn't help but notice he got just as many messages from his not-quite-ex-wife. Adrian and I had been in a cold war since I'd last turned him down and he'd decided to go on a date with Lisa. We interacted professionally all day, but we were chilly to each other outside of the room. He'd abruptly dropped his pursuit of me. This was a good thing, I told myself. My integrity would remain intact. Unfortunately, rather than abating, my pain was now raging. I was stuck with him in that airless room all day and most of the night, hopelessly smitten. On breaks, I'd write in my journal, trying to deconstruct my psyche. What was the matter with me? Was this really about him, or about losing out to that girl? Honest scrutiny led me to believe his relationship with Lisa stung, but my craziness over him had predated her. In the writers' room, I kept up my detached air, but I sometimes slipped out of the room to weep secretly in my office. I was disgusted at myself for wasting this emotion over him. I was amazed at the ferocity of my suffering, yet at no point did I connect it to the pain I was feeling over my mother.

At the end of the week Lisa made an appearance in the writers' wing. After spending a good deal of time behind closed doors in Adrian's office, she made a beeline for mine. She waltzed in and shut the door behind her. This took me by surprise. Since the actors' arrival at work, she and I had had minimal interaction, and when we had spoken, the tone had been merely civil. Now Lisa sat on my sofa and asked with affected brightness how my time at the show had been so far. How did I like the writers? Did I like any of them in particular? Her gaze was direct. Not even a thin, wispy veil hung over the fact that she was asking about my relationship with Adrian. I deflected, steering the conversation toward people we'd had in common years ago. I told her Jonathan was now engaged, his wedding set for the spring. Before she could get me back on track, a PA knocked and said she was needed in Makeup.

She left and I shut the door behind her. I sat back down at my desk and then there was another knock. Adrian entered, shutting the door behind him, his face flushed.

"What did she say to you?"

"What do you care? What the hell is going on?"

Adrian sat on the edge of the sofa. He launched into an emotional monologue about how the silence between us was killing him. He said all he talked about with Lisa was me, which had rightly made her suspicious.

"You're perfect for me—you're like a Winona Ryder who reads. I can't be with her—she swims with dolphins on cable! Please, please meet me outside of work for lunch, breakfast, anything."

And with that, I yielded.

FIVE

did not tell my mother I was dating my boss, and when I took the inspirational quotes off the walls, she just assumed I'd finished some script or other I'd been working on. She'd recently developed mouth sores from chemo, which were painful and made it difficult to eat. Andrea, the oncological nurse, told her that rinsing her mouth with saltwater might help, so every thirty minutes, around the clock, my mother shuffled off to Barrow Street's little bathroom to rinse out her mouth. It did not help, but my mother never gave up hope. My new secret romance was having a blissful, druglike effect on me and took the edge off of those long nights. It was a scary kind of drug—like heroin. A crash was inevitable.

My mother had an escape of her own that buoyed her spirits and helped take her mind off her illness: the building of her dream house. She had grown up poor on the outskirts of Beverly Hills and spent her childhood looking with longing at the mansions just a few streets north but far out of reach. She'd vowed that one day she would live in a house like that. At the height of their marriage, my parents had bought a large modern house that brought her closer to her dream. Upon their divorce, they sold it, making a good profit. My mother took her share of the money, bought a piece of land on a hill in the most inexpensive part of Southampton (north of the highway, deep in the woods), and set about building the biggest, grandest house on the street. She planted a velvety lawn and enclosed it with a white picket fence to match the picture she'd been carrying in her head since she was a little girl. Construction of the house had been completed right before her ovarian cancer diagnosis. Now she was consumed by choosing the countertops, cabinets, moldings, sinks.

Since my mother did not sleep, she welcomed the sun and was up and about by seven. She'd deliberate over the design options for her house and was in the habit of talking to me as though I were awake, whatever the hour. She'd drop four squares of tile onto the comforter, all slightly different shades of beige: "Which do you like for the master bathroom? The one with the trim?" She treated each tile, each swatch of fabric, with a tender love. Nothing gave her greater joy than stumbling upon the right doorknob or light fixture. The house was more than the realization of a lifelong dream—it filled an emotional abyss that had its roots in childhood deprivation. In the dead of night, my mother talked about her house in amazement. "It's everything I ever hoped for. It seems too good to be true." The tears would flow. "Maybe it *is* too good to be true. Maybe God thinks I don't deserve it and that's why he gave me cancer."

I hugged her and insisted, "Mom, no. God would never want to punish you." My words provided no comfort.

From the moment I met Adrian at a West Village café for our first proper date, I found myself in the throes of a passionate affair.

He made me feel intensely alive—a vivid contrast to the nights spent wading in the topic of death.

Adrian wanted to be up-front at work and tell everyone we were dating, but I did not. I knew the fallout for me would be severe, and I held out hope that it could be avoided by keeping the relationship a secret. That was unbearably naive. We were in a room together, with six other people, for up to fourteen hours a day. Poker was not my game. Later, a coworker painted a picture of how I appeared to others in the writers' room: "You were like that cartoon of Snow White. Every time Adrian spoke, the music swelled and little bluebirds appeared around your head."

While I was busy swooning, resentments about our relationship were brewing. Ominous signs about Adrian also began to crop up. A friend of a friend who knew him from Los Angeles passed on the information that he'd had several affairs before he'd separated from his wife, calling him a "sleazy cheater."

When my mother was away in Southampton, I spent every night with him. I didn't know what I was doing. I didn't know why I was doing it. Every morning I'd tell myself this was the day I would put an end to it, and every day I would fail. I called my old therapist Dr. Mark Epstein, made an appointment, and told him that I was in trouble.

Before Mark had a chance to help, the first bomb hit. It was November: the point in the season when each writer's option was up for renewal. The scandal unfolded just as I'd feared. A studio executive in California made a call to the creators of our show— someone had reported our relationship. Because Adrian was my direct boss, the studio was afraid of potential lawsuits.

My agent, Jeff Wise, was also my dear friend. He'd taken a chance on me when I was nothing more than an unemployed actress who'd typed up a few measly spec scripts. Before I'd earned him a cent, Jeff and his wife would have me over for dinner, and I'd often babysit for their infant son. Jeff and I were close. I'd normally tell him everything that was going on in my life. This time, he'd been informed of my behavior by the studio executive. He was disappointed and livid.

"You're a great writer, Jessica—you've got everything going for you. How could you compromise your career this way? And why didn't you tell me immediately so I could begin damage control?"

I was guilty and ashamed and had no answer. Remarkably, Adrian and I were not fired, and once we were out of the closet, people at work acted—at least outwardly—nonchalant about the situation. Our relationship continued.

The second bomb exploded just before Christmas. Adrian always maintained that his divorce was imminent, even though his wife was unhappy about it. He painted her as unstable and hysterical. He'd moved out of the family house and into his own apartment in Los Angeles eight months before he'd taken this job in New York. At first, whenever he was in California for a weekend visiting his kids, he called me at the end of the night from his apartment. Lately, he'd taken to calling me during the day; at night his phone would be shut off. I suspected he was with his wife. He denied it.

I was strung out like a junkie. Adrian and I were writing a movie together outside of work, and our creative partnership was an additional barbiturate. He'd begun talking about us moving to Venice, California, when the show ended; we'd live together, write films, and have a kid. The kid was my stipulation; even in my trance, I was firm in my desire to have children. My best friends had met him by now and were horrified. I assured them and Mark Epstein that I knew this was not a man I'd grow old with—inevitably he'd cheat on me, chuck me aside for the next woman—but I thought he could be faithful for about a decade, and I felt so *alive* with him. I used the analogy of Sean Penn. I posed the question to my girlfriends: What would you do if Sean Penn focused all of his intense, sexy, unstable energy on *you*, declared his love for you, wanted to live together in a shack by the sea? You'd know the chances of rocking on a porch swing with him at eighty were nil, but could you pass up the ride? They gawked at me like I was certifiable. Mark Epstein suggested I double up on my therapy sessions. My friends swarmed behind my back, planning an intervention, but they would never get the chance.

One afternoon at work, Adrian took a call from his wife and spontaneously told her about our relationship. She was extremely upset. It came out that my suspicions had been founded—Adrian had been sleeping with her in Los Angeles while he and I had been involved. "All of that's in the past now," Adrian offered, trying to assuage me. "We're finally free to move on with our lives."

I went to the bathroom and threw up. Suddenly, I related to this woman. I felt terrible for her. She was my age. She was a mother with four children. We were talking about a man who would never be good for anyone. You'd think I would have summoned my strength and left him, told him to go back to his wife, his children, his responsibilities. That I did not do.

That night, Adrian and I went to a restaurant on Tenth Avenue. He was giddy with freedom. His characteristic lack of empathy was on rare display. His coldness toward his wife was scary, sadistic. I was shell-shocked. He told me he felt like it was our wedding night. I flatly reminded him that he'd lied to me. Cheated on me. He apologized but replied that getting out of a marriage was always messy.

Our Christmas break was upon us, and Adrian was going to Los Angeles for two weeks to see his children. He begged me to come with him. My mother was scheduled for surgery, which meant I would be staying in New York. I told him in no uncertain terms that I would not stand for abuse. We would wipe the slate clean with the understanding that he had no room for error. If he lied to me or betrayed me, it would be over.

In therapy, I described how I'd laid down the law with Adrian. Mark listened in silence. When I was through, he took a beat, then asked if I thought I was creating turmoil in my personal life to distract myself from what was going on with my mother. It was my turn to be silent. I had no answer. After a while, Mark said matter-of-factly: "Your mother is going to die from cancer, Jessica. There is nothing you can do but bear witness."

Early the next morning, Adrian took a cab to JFK to catch a JetBlue flight to Long Beach, while my dad's driver picked up my mother, my sister, and me to take us to the hospital. My dad was already in the passenger seat, and my parents' two elderly black Labs were also packed into the car. The driver drove the dogs around Manhattan all day, every day, in a black Hummer. Once in the morning and once in the afternoon he'd take the dogs running in the park; the rest of the time they lounged on the backseat as the car circled city blocks. Ostensibly, my father had a driver to pick up clients, but all human passengers had to perch on the edge of the seat while the dogs spread out like royalty. "I used to have a Lincoln Town Car," my father would tell his befuddled clients, with his customary bravado. "but with two big dogs, I decided I needed a Hummer." Though my parents were divorced, they remained close.

My mother's operation was for a hernia. Her extensive stomach surgery had been just over a year ago, and we were told it was not uncommon for a hernia to occur after that kind of internal disruption. Apparently, this operation would be simple. It was what they might discover once they opened her up that was frightening.

My mom was dressed in a gray velvet sweat suit, with a gray cashmere blanket over her shoulders. Her hair was now all silvery gray, with brown remnants at the very ends. Her face was as beautiful as ever, though it had aged dramatically over the past year. She was animated and childlike in the car. She had packed a bag and said she'd included two sets of matching nighties and silk robes—one pale pink, and one lavender. "I like to be pretty till the last minute."

My sister's boyfriend, Bruce, met us at the front doors of the hospital with two dozen fat yellow roses for my mom. She glowed at the sight of him and the roses. It was six a.m. and Bruce had driven all the way in from Southampton, where he lived, to wish her well.

My dad, Danielle, and I sat with Mom in the tiny dressing room before surgery. She made Danielle grab a handful of the thin cotton hospital gowns so she could choose the one she liked. She explained her selection process to us as she rooted through the gowns. "Some of them are gargantuous; some of them have rips, see? I like the ones with the smaller pattern, like this. They're more feminine."

My mother held the blue gauzy surgery cap in her hand until the nurse called her name. Unlike the last surgery, when she was wheeled on a gurney, this time she walked down the long hall to her operating room. She turned around, cap on her head, and waved good-bye to us. She was crying. So were Danielle and I. My dad sat on a plastic chair and read the paper. Whenever my mother was in the hospital, my father would be there, but his emotions were tightly bottled.

After several hours, the surgeon came out and said the operation had been a success. They took a wash to test for cancer, but he could not see any tumors with the naked eye. We were elated.

Adrian called in the afternoon to see how the operation went, and we said we'd speak that evening. My mom was brought up from recovery to her private room. She had a fever. Danielle and I took turns placing cool washcloths on her head, neck, and chest and fed her ice chips. The hours went by; Adrian did not call. Danielle and I were up all night tending to our mother, and when it was past midnight in Los Angeles I understood what was going on. I had told my friends I thought Adrian could be faithful for ten years. In reality, he could not last one night.

By the morning, my mother's fever had broken and mine had begun. I was burning up and I had a sore throat. They sent me home from the hospital so that I would not get my mother sick. Adrian called dozens of times over the next few days, but I did not pick up and would not pick up for the next two weeks. Though my self-esteem was tattered, I had enough left to end things. I fired off an e-mail: "We're through. Stay away from me." The following day I had a 102-degree fever and strep throat. I was too weak to hail a taxi, so the driver, the dogs, and my dad picked me up. My dad took me to my doctor's appointment like he had when I was a little girl. By the time the Christmas break was over and we returned to work, Adrian was back together with his wife.

There were two and a half months left in the television season. After a week of icy silence, Adrian redeclared his feelings for me and continued to bat me around like a trapped mouse for the remaining days. With the help of Mark Epstein, I made it to March without ever seeing Adrian outside of work. When the job ended, I changed all of my phone numbers. I never spoke to him again.

SIX

March 2003

My mother sat on the crunchy white paper of the examining table and the doctor sat on a stool. We were on the chemo floor of the NYU hospital, far from the wing that housed the doctor's more reassuringly furnished office. Danielle and I had been called in to discuss the future course of our mom's chemotherapy.

For a year, she'd been on both Carboplatin and Doxil. In January she'd reached the maximum dose of carbo a human being can tolerate, so it had been removed from her regimen. Now it looked as if the Doxil had also run its course. A side effect of Doxil was skin toxicity, and my mother's symptoms had grown severe: sores in her mouth and in her rectum, chapped hands and feet that had cracked open in wounds. The doctor told us he wanted to change tracks and put her on a new drug called Gemzar. This broached a delicate issue. Though Gemzar did not cause total hair loss, it did cause hair thinning.

My mom's eyes clouded with tears. Her voice was childlike.

"No. I won't lose my hair, I won't do it."

The doctor tried to gently assuage her. "Gemzar will not cause you to lose all your hair, Stephanie."

"I told all of you from the beginning that I won't do this, so don't pressure me. I love my hair. It's thick and gorgeous. What am I going to have, bald patches?"

"Usually the hair thins quite evenly. It will be thinner, that's all. And in some cases the side effect never occurs."

The tears spilled over.

"Oh, it'll occur for me. With my luck. Will it be so thin you can see through to the scalp?"

"In some cases."

"No. I won't do it."

Danielle and I jumped all over her. "Mommy, if this is the right drug, you have to do it. Thin hair isn't the end of the world. We'll buy you new wigs if you don't feel comfortable."

My mother's expression turned grim, her face streaked with tears. Her voice was bitter, but she wanted to live. "Back to the wigs."

TWO WEEKS LATER, on one of the first warm spring afternoons of the year, my mother and I walked across Christopher Street toward Seventh Avenue south. The day was sparkling, the trees newly green. My mother carried a wig head covered by long, swinging brunette hair. We ambled slowly, my arm linked through hers as a gesture of endearment, but also to support her. My mom was smiling and chatty. She'd spent about ten days mourning her possible hair loss and then put it behind her. Always forward-thinking, she was now on to the project of creating a new "fabulous wig," and we were en route to the hair stylist.

"Do you think I should keep the wig long or cut it shoulder-length? One good thing about wearing a wig is that I can have my brown hair back without those toxic dyes. I tore out a picture from a magazine of Goldie Hawn's haircut to show Amir. I'll be the only bald woman in a wig to still look like a movie star!"

She was animated and giggly, flushed with the happiness of being alive. The salon was an unassuming little place my sister had discovered. Danielle and I frequently dropped in to have our hair blown dry by a sweet gay Israeli man named Amir. (Once I'd started working professionally as a writer, I wanted a more adult, polished look. The first shift in my appearance was taming my abundant, unruly hair.) After hearing our raves, our mom started going to Amir, too. The place was owned by a robust Italian named Vito, and the stylists ran the gamut of local color. It had the familiarity of a small-town beauty parlor—everybody knew us there. My mother and I and the wig head made our entrance. We were greeted warmly from all sides.

"Stephanie, Jessica, how are you? Stephanie, you look beautiful! Where's Danielle? What is that wig?"

My mother planted the wig head in the center of Amir's station and the three of us stood around it. My mother pulled visual aids out of her purse: the photo of Goldie and several snapshots of herself, precancer, when her hair had been in its full glory.

"I'm on this new chemo and they say my hair is going to thin, how much God only knows, so I want a smashing wig just in case. I tried on the wigs from my last cancer and they just seem too wiggy. You know I only like long hair—I never let my girls cut their hair short—so I only want to trim it, but I don't want the cut to feel heavy. You see how Goldie has the length while it's still bouncy in front?"

Amir had his own wig stand at the shop, so we left the hair

and exited, my mom carrying her wig head under her arm like a football.

My ex-boyfriend Jonathan the playwright was getting married in a few weeks, and my mother had recently helped me choose an outfit for the wedding. She'd sat in a chair in the Calvin Klein store on Madison Avenue as I'd modeled an array of dresses. When I was young, she'd drag me shopping and dress me up in clothes that had nothing to do with my personality. She'd ambush me with her taste, and I'd leave the store weighted down with shopping bags and feeling emotionally drained. Our recent Calvin Klein shopping excursion had a very different tenor. My mom was sick, and I felt lucky to have her with me; I found comfort in the familiarity of the scene. As a child, going shopping with my mom had felt like an arduous chore; now it felt nurturing. Many other factors were also converging. As my mother's illness progressed, my need to rebel against her and her material-girl persona waned. As my mother's humanity shone through, her love of fine clothes became merely an endearing detail of her personality. I was also now a thirty-three-year-old career woman—my tastes were changing and inching closer to hers. The bohemian thrift-store look felt juvenile to me and had lost its appeal.

I had chosen a pair of dangling earrings to wear with the dress, so after leaving Amir's, the next task of the day was to get my left ear pierced. I rarely wore jewelry and when I tried to put the earrings in, I discovered one ear had closed. As we crossed the street, I told my mom I was heading to one of those tattoo parlors on Eighth Street and she insisted on coming with me. This never would have happened before my mother got sick; she would have been much too busy to keep me company on this sort of mundane errand.

My elegant, bejeweled mother sat in a chair in the tattoo parlor, the wig head on her lap, while a squat, bald man with bulging muscles so cartoonish he could have been the strong man in a circus led me to the piercing stool. He was covered in tattoos, and though he looked like someone who would part the sea of bodies in the yard at Rikers, his manner was gentle. Two young girls with piercings in their eyebrows, noses, belly buttons, and along the lengths of their ears waited in line for their turn on the stool. One girl was there to get her tongue pierced and the other was debating whether she should do it, too. The Strong Man swabbed my ear with alcohol and my mother asked if I wanted to grab a bite to eat after. "Sure," I said. "Where would you like to go?"

"I don't care. I just want to be with you."

As the Strong Man shot a metal stud through my ear, I looked at my mom, unfazed by her surroundings, eyes focused on me like a bear guarding her cub. Cancer and chemo were aging her and she seemed frail, but more to the point, I was struck by the shift in her energy toward me. Gradually and without my noticing, she had grown genuinely maternal.

A WEEK LATER, Danielle, my mother, and I were back on the chemo floor for round two of Gemzar. Edgy and upset, my mother clutched a notepad on which she'd written down all of her symptoms and complaints. She told Andrea the nurse that her hair had begun to shed, leaving a wispy trail on the floor behind her. But even worse, she'd started having trouble eating. Small bites of food sometimes caused her to double over in pain, and often she would vomit her food right back up. Even water could be hard to get down. Usually, she was nauseous for only one or two days directly after receiving the drugs, but this sickness came on two weeks after she'd gotten chemo. Andrea listened carefully and asked if this had become a consistent reaction to food or only sometimes. "Only sometimes," my mother replied. "Other times I can eat and I'm fine." Andrea said it seemed as though my mom's bowel was inflamed (from tumor, she meant, though she did not say it). As long as the problem was intermittent, it suggested she probably would not have to undergo surgery to remove a blockage.

The word *surgery* sent chills through my mother. Andrea asked about her sores and skin chafing, a topic that further depressed her. Although she had stopped taking Doxil, there had been no improvement. "I rinse my mouth out with saltwater a hundred times a day—it does nothing. I go through bottles of lotion on my hands and feet—it seems to make them worse."

Out of the blue, my mother's eyes lit up a bit. She asked Andrea if she was allowed to travel. As long as it didn't interfere with her treatment, Andrea said, sure. My mother turned to me and Danielle and told us she'd been thinking about the things she'd always wanted to do and realized she'd better do them now. In fact, she'd already chosen the first one:

"It's a dream of mine to see Céline Dion perform live—I read that she has a new show. Girls, we're going to Vegas."

SEVEN

The trip was arranged so that my mother could spend a few days in her hometown, Los Angeles, before heading to Vegas to see Céline Dion perform at Caesars Palace. I had taken repossession of the Hollywood Hills guest house, but the cozy one-room cottage was too small for me, my mother, and Danielle. Besides which, it was perched on the top of a hill and required climbing thirty stone steps to reach the front door—not an option for my mom. My mother's oldest childhood friend (and next-door neighbor), Roberta, had moved to the other side of the proverbial tracks—she now lived in the fancy part of Beverly Hills. It was decided that I would stay in the guest house, while Danielle and my mother stayed with Roberta.

Roberta is rail thin, her hair raven black, her skin soapy white, and her lips perpetually bright with pink or red lipstick. My mother often remarked that Roberta was in a time warp: She dressed in tight, tiny getups like she was still in high school, had a cheerleader's "rah, rah!" personality, and talked about their girl-hood adventures as if they'd happened yesterday. Roberta was a housewife who would occasionally moonlight as a nurse; she had a simple sweetness and adored my mother. Her favorite hobby was line dancing, which she did religiously every week, dressed in a cowgirl outfit. Roberta lived in a doll's house in Beverly Hills—literally. She had a vast collection of china dolls that were displayed in glass cases in every room.

My mother was ecstatic to be back in Los Angeles. She rented a car and drove me and Danielle around the neighborhood where she grew up. "That's my high school, Hamilton High—I used to cut school all the time and go to the beach. I'd throw my bathing suit on and drive barefoot—I always drove barefoot. I'm a real California girl!"

Roberta and my mother had gotten married on the exact same day in 1965, and they left their husbands around the same time thirty-five years later. Roberta was now dating a real estate agent named John whom she'd met line dancing. Once back in LA, my mother's dream house in Southampton seemed to fade from her memory. All she could see was home. "I love California—what if I move back? I never meant to live my whole life in New York."

At my mother's urging, we piled into John's car one afternoon to go on an unlikely house-hunting expedition. After showing us a couple of duds, John brought us to a beauty with sweeping views in Marina Del Ray. My mother was suffering from stomach pain that day and had trouble climbing the stairs to the second floor, though she pushed herself. Once upstairs, Roberta leaned on the window ledge in her teeny jean skirt and turned to my mom with bright eyes: "So, Steffy, what do you think?" My mother was mesmerized. In the moment, everything else had fallen away—her house, her doctors, her chemo treatments, her cancer. She was temporarily lost in a fantasy of the future. For a moment, we all blocked out reality and joined her. She turned to Roberta, full of wonder: "I love it. My girls and I can live here on the beach. I can finally come home."

Calista Flockhart is one of my best friends from my theater days, and my mother hadn't seen her since she'd moved to California and adopted a baby. We scheduled a time for me and my mom to drive over for a visit. Calista lived with her boyfriend, the actor Harrison Ford, but I didn't expect him to be there. We had been hanging out with Calista and her son for about an hour when Harrison walked into the den and joined us. He knew my mother was ill. She was curled up in an overstuffed armchair, wearing her new wig. He sat down on a sofa right beside her. He turned his full attention to my mother as if no one else existed, asking her questions about her business and her new house. My mother transformed into a blushing ingenue before our eyes. She spoke coquettishly about the antique dishes and Depression-era glassware she stocked in her store. As she described the room in her house she'd built solely for the purpose of hosing down her dogs, she giggled and tilted her head demurely. When it was time to leave, Harrison Ford escorted my mother to the car and held the door open for her like a proper suitor. I will never forget what a gentleman he was. For the rest of the day and night, my mother forgot her stomach pain and hair loss and mouth sores—that day, she was a princess.

The next morning, Danielle and I took our mother to Cedars Sinai for her next chemotherapy session. She'd begged for a chemo vacation, but her CA-125 numbers had been rising and her doctor felt that missing even one treatment was not an option.

THE LAS VEGAS TRIP was to be an extravaganza—no expense spared. I suspect my mother chose the Venetian from all the hotels on the Strip because it housed a branch of Canyon Ranch—a spa famous for its fitness programs. The Canyon Ranch in Tucson, Arizona, was my mother's favorite place in the world. Though she could no longer partake in spinning or step classes, she liked the idea that there was a Canyon Ranch right in our very hotel.

My mom rented a lavish suite and invited Roberta and her daughter, Robyn, to join us. Robyn, in contrast to her mother, dressed in conservative, preppy clothing. She worked as a nutritionist at Cedars Sinai and had a vanity plate on her car that read FAT FREE. Like Roberta, Robyn loved my mother. Over the past few years, she had made annual trips to New York to spend a few days with her in Southampton, biking and Rollerblading.

We arrived in Vegas the night before the main event—Céline Dion's concert, *A New Day*. The show had been sold out for months; it had required a lot of effort and many connections to snag five house seats, and the tickets cost a fortune. My mother and Roberta were giddy about seeing Céline Dion live; Robyn seemed a bit excited; Danielle and I cared to see Céline Dion about as much as we would have cared to see Wayne Newton—that is, not at all—but we were thrilled that our mother was happy. We were also relieved that we'd pulled the whole thing off.

In our suite, there were two king-size beds and a cot. Robyn and Roberta claimed one of the kings, Danielle took the cot, and my mother and I were back in our role as bedfellows. Before falling asleep, my mother chattered on about all the different kinds of food she was craving. "A hamburger's floating before my eyes," she said. "Tomorrow I want a hamburger at the Hard Rock Cafe. . . ." In the past week my mother had scarcely been able to eat. Nibbling on a piece of bread could trigger violent stomach pain and land her on the bathroom floor, head hung over the toilet. She'd always loved food, but now she was obsessed. At heart she was an optimist; she believed that tomorrow this problem would pass and she'd be able to eat again, so she planned her fantasy meals. My mother's stomach was once again distended and had grown to an alarming size. As she lay there, talking to me about noodle kugel, fierce gurgling sounds rose from her belly. "Hear that?" she would ask. "That's not normal."

The Big Day arrived. Danielle and I lounged around the room, keeping my mother company as she rested up for the evening's event. My mother made us try on all the outfits we had brought so she could tell us which she liked best. She happily chattered on about how we all had to look *gorgeous* for the show. My mother had not eaten in days; that afternoon she asked Robyn to bring her some chicken broth. She took a few swallows of soup. It might as well have been poison. She was overtaken with nausea and a stabbing pain. Danielle held her hair back as she retched in the toilet. In between gasps she insisted: "I'm going to see Céline no matter what." She stood up. She pulled on a pair of leggings and a black stretch tank top with a silver embroidered dragon studded with rhinestones. "You can't go to the concert if you're sick," we told her. "Please, lie down. Relax." But my mother wouldn't hear of it. She clung to the walls as she made her way back to the bathroom to put on the wig-concoction of ponytail and bangs sewn into a baseball cap. "I'm green—I can't even put on my makeup—I don't care. I came all the way to Las Vegas and I'm not going to miss Céline Dion." This painful scene continued for another forty-five minutes. Finally, back on the bathroom floor, my mother admitted defeat. She started hollering at the rest of us to hurry, otherwise we would all miss the concert. When we insisted on staying with her, she became hysterical and swore she'd never forgive us if we did not go see Céline. She allowed only Roberta to remain behind and pushed me, Danielle, and Robyn out the door.

We entered the mayhem of Caesars Palace in stunned silence. A mother and daughter were trying to buy tickets from a scalper; we amazed them by handing over our two extras and refused to accept money. The mother thanked us and said it was a special gift because her daughter had just recovered from brain cancer.

Our seats were fantastic—seventh row center. The show began with an explosion of blue—a vista of feathers and flashing lights. Céline Dion alighted, her voice filling the arena, and Danielle and I began to sob. In the middle of the second song, Danielle had an idea. She turned on her cell phone and dialed our mother. The call went through and remained connected. Our mother and Roberta took turns listening to Céline Dion live from her bed in the Venetian.

That night in the dark, my mother lay awake next to me; her energy was very different. She was quiet and loving. She said it had been a mistake to travel, that this would be her last trip. She told me she knew she didn't have much longer to live. I began to cry, and then she cried, too. But for the first time in our late-night talks, she focused solely on providing me, her child, with comfort. "God gives and he takes away. He *does*. He'll give you a baby, Jessica. Like you've always wanted. He'll give you someone to love. And I'll always be with you."

The next day, my mother possessed an unfamiliar calm. Robyn and Roberta had taken an early-morning flight back to Los Angeles, leaving the three of us alone. My mother linked arms with me and Danielle, and we strolled slowly past the gondolas and other Vegas-style approximations of Venice. She would gaze at one of us for a long time, then turn and look at the other. She kept saying, "I'm so *lucky*. I have the best girls in the world." She said that she was finally at peace because last night she realized that she would not outlive her money. "Whatever happens now, I'll be okay."

EIGHT

pon her return to New York, my mother was diagnosed with an ileus: a paralysis of the bowel. The cancer had caused her intestines to slow down. Yet some days she was able to digest food without pain and nausea, so it was not considered an obstruction and surgery was put off.

Because my mother's CA-125 numbers were steadily rising, my father took her to see a famed oncologist for a second opinion. The doctor had studied her records before their arrival. Without much preamble, he told them squarely that chemotherapy was no longer having any useful effect. In his estimation, my mother's cancer was too developed for help. His advice: She should cease treatment and try to enjoy her remaining days.

"How long would I have to live?" she asked.

"Approximately three months."

This was a shocking number. A year and a half ago she had been given five years. My parents sat in numb silence, tears streaming down my mother's face. The doctor placed a hand on her shoulder and walked out of the office.

My mother stuck with her original doctor and continued chemo treatments. Aside from the intermittent inability to eat, she was living a relatively normal life. She was still able to drive to the Hamptons, walk her Labrador in Central Park, and run her business. She hired an au pair named Jolie from Krakow, Poland, to help take care of her house. Jolie arrived in New York with no idea that my mother was ill. She gazed up at the skyscrapers in wonder, and it filled my mother with joy to usher her around Manhattan. My mom promised to show Jolie *everything*—Chinatown, SoHo, the Met. However, my mom told her, they would be spending most of their time in Southampton. She wanted to have the most wonderful summer at her house: planting flowers, walking on the beach, enjoying every moment.

On June 20, 2003, two weeks into my mother's idyllic summer, she was rushed to the hospital: emergency surgery for high-grade small bowel obstruction. After the operation, she woke up in a daze, turned to me, Danielle, and our dad, and said: "Is this all okay . . . ? I just want to be safe." It was not okay. She had a fever of 103 and an infection. A horrible odor emitted from her wound: I recognized it instantly as the smell from Harriette's deathbed. The surgeon told us there was a strong possibility that my mother had a hole in her intestine, but because her intestine was encased in disease a hole would be impossible to fix. He attached a clear bag to the wound and instructed our mother to drink thick, dark liquid charcoal. This was a test: If the charcoal appeared in the bag, we would know there was a hole, and our mother's life would end in a matter of days. Our mom was too high on morphine to grasp what was happening, but she had a panic attack when we tried to get her to drink the terrible mixture. She was nauseated and claustrophobic and insisted she didn't want it. Somehow, we persuaded her to get it down. Danielle and I spent the most harrowing night looking for the charcoal. Danielle's boyfriend, Bruce, was also there. The charcoal never appeared—we were granted a reprieve. Even the nurse on our floor, Patty, wept for joy. The next day, our mom went back into surgery to have the infected fluid drained. When she healed, there would be no more chemo. She would return home to her dream house in Southampton under palliative care. East End Hospice would dispatch nurses to help her die in as much comfort as possible.

In the days before her discharge, my mother sat up in the hospital bed, looking like a wide-eyed little girl. The brutal effects of the surgeries had knocked any worldliness out of her. She no longer had the filter that exists between impression and response. She had no more agendas. Her energy was open and vulnerable, her reactions pure as water. When Danielle or I entered the room saying, "Hi, Mommy," her face would light up with joy. When a nurse she liked came in to check on her, she was full of uncontainable smiles. Her beauty had intensified. Rather than being just a pretty woman, she glowed from within. Sometimes she would remember her circumstance and get scared about going home. One night she cried because she'd wanted to plant gardens at her house and she feared she wouldn't be alive to see everything in bloom.

When Danielle and Bruce drove my mother up the hill to her house in Southampton, she gasped. The once-bare driveway was lined with blossoming trees. Mounds of flowers bowed lightly in the breeze. Bruce had landscaped her property as a present for her homecoming. She pressed her face up against the window, smiling and blinking her eyes, and said, "I feel like I'm in a dream."

· · · ·

AFTER HER DIVORCE, my mom had scoured Southampton for an affordable piece of land upon which to build her house. She found the three hilltop acres with a view of the Peconic Bay, and cried, "This is it! This spot has wonderful karma!" The land was owned by an attractive young man whose primary business was building ten-million-dollar spec houses in town. After charming him into selling her the land at a discount, my mother continued to call him for advice on construction matters. They became friends, and he told her he was single—did she have any daughters? As it happened, Danielle's occupation was building spec houses in North Carolina—with her husband. Though Danielle was the natural match, I was the single daughter, so my mother called to set me up on a blind date for the very first time: "His name is Bruce and he's *fabulous.*" Family lore has it that I stood Bruce up twice, though I remember canceling on him only once. Around this time, Danielle left her husband and moved back to New York. One afternoon, Dani stopped by Bruce's construction site with our mom and expertly talked shop. "This tall, gorgeous blond started quoting the price of sheetrock," Bruce would later recall. "I was in love." Dani was in the process of divorcing and not ready to get involved with anyone. However, she did need a job. Danielle worked for Bruce's company for six months before finally agreeing to a date with him. Just as they became a couple, our mother grew seriously ill. Dani and Bruce lived in Southampton full-time, as did our mother (when she wasn't in New York seeing doctors or doing stints in the hospital). Danielle's professional duties waned as her caretaking duties increased. Soon enough, she stopped working altogether.

MY MOTHER bounced back so vigorously from her June operations that we allowed ourselves a bit of denial about the meaning of the

hospice nurses. We pretended they were there to make her better.
My mom moved slowly, but she was always moving. She taught
Jolie how to iron sheets perfectly. She cooked beautiful meals,
though she could only nibble at solid food. Her happiness at being
in her house—and being showered with attention from her daughters—gave her a sparkle that could be mistaken for health. For a
few weeks, Danielle and I went back to believing she would defy
the odds and live a year or two. By August, that illusion vanished,
and she began to deteriorate rapidly.

In June I'd been offered a writing job on a new show in California. I accepted it with trepidation, telling myself I could quit
and move home at a moment's notice. Almost immediately I took
Fridays off and flew to New York every weekend. Still, there was
some tension between me and Danielle. She was bearing the
greater burden of our mother's illness. Two months in, when my
mother's condition sharply worsened, I left the show and moved
into the Southampton house.

In the few weeks on this job, I had been pursued romantically
by another coworker. Jason was a handful of years younger than
I, and worked as the writers' assistant. My rebuffs were sweet
but condescending: "What are you thinking? I'm way too old
for you. . . ." Jason would not be deterred—he flirted, courted,
cajoled. Jason was the antithesis of Adrian. His overtures were
heartbreakingly earnest and a sharp contrast to Adrian's cynical
machinations. Jason knew my mother was ill and that I was vulnerable; he maneuvered me out of harm's way in our office, which
was a thicket of politics. He had the blond, fresh-faced good looks
of the actors who starred on WB shows. Jason was undeniably
attractive, good, and kind, yet he lived like a frat boy with a
roommate and beer bottles and empty pizza boxes. I doubted we
would make a lasting couple. I thought about Mark Epstein's in-

sight about how I had created havoc in my personal life to distract myself from pain. Giving in to Jason felt like I'd once again be permitting myself an indulgence, an escape, but Jason was a good guy. As long as we were straight with each other, what would be the harm? I agreed to go with him to the movies. That was our only date before I moved to Southampton. Nevertheless, he became my long-distance boyfriend.

Jason was not faint of heart. He jumped right into the fray, listening to me cry for hours, day or night, as I narrated the most awful scenes. Through each horror, he was always on the other end of the line, keeping me company, offering comfort.

My mother was on a host of medicines. Danielle and I doled out pills every four hours and checked off what she'd taken on a chart taped to the wall. She wore fentanyl patches on the back of her shoulder that needed to be changed every two days. One of us would tear the used ones off like a Band-Aid, wipe the area with adhesive remover, swab it with alcohol prep, and apply new ones. My mother would badger us to make sure we flushed the old patches down the toilet so the dogs wouldn't eat them and get high.

The fentanyl had begun to slur my mother's words. She puttered around the house, tipsy from the drugs, calling herself "a drunken sailor." Her sentences became more fragmented, though she could be extremely charming, even funny. When she couldn't summon the word she wanted, she waved her arms in broad flourishes. Almost every day she wore her black tank top with the silver rhinestoned dragon. She said the dragon was "eating up the cancer." She was always on the move. One of us would inevitably encourage her to sit down and rest, and she'd say, "I'm a jumping bean, that's just who I am." She loved her house so; she lingered in each room, admiring it. "I love the kitchen, the porch, the garden. I'm very well-rounded." She insisted on doing everything for herself. Once I found her in the bathroom, squatting with great difficulty, trying to reach the Listerine.

"Mom, why didn't you ask me for help?"

"I don't want to be helpless."

Suddenly, she realized she was stuck and could not stand up.

"Help me!"

As I struggled to lift her, she shouted, "Pull! Pull!"

"I'm trying. I'm not as strong as Hercules, you know."

"Then weight-lift! Weight-lift!"

Another time I found her gazing out the bathroom window. "What are you looking for?" I asked.

"The sun."

Nights were unbearable. My mother felt the changes in her body and was terrified to sleep. She was afraid she'd stop breathing and never wake up. Every time she drifted off, she'd jolt herself out of it, gasping with fright. Often she would make one of us hold her arm while she paced. "Must keep walking," she would mumble. Otherwise, she insisted on sitting upright on the edge of the bed with her feet touching the floor. She felt certain that death would come in sleep, so she was hell-bent on staying awake. "I'm scared to die," she would say. "Where will I go?"

During the day she wanted to be with me or my sister at every moment. She would stand facing me and stare into my eyes for long stretches of time—an uncomfortably intense exercise. Before her illness, she never maintained eye contact when talking; now she couldn't get enough of it. "I just love looking at you," she would say. "I know one thing I did right. I raised two wonderful girls." As the days marched on, she would cry frequently and talk about her death. She craved constant physical affection. One day she hugged me, tears rolling down her cheeks: "I don't have many hugs left to give." She looked at me with piercing eyes and said, "Never forget me, Jessica."

My mother loved food, and her inability to eat caused her great anguish. Her diet now consisted of baby sips of Enlive and the occasional orange soda. On brave days she took minuscule bites of food like hamburger or toast, knowing she would pay for it dearly, winding up in agony, retching on the bathroom floor. She had started fantasizing about food in Vegas; she continued to do so for the rest of her life. Each day she fixated on a certain dish, often from her childhood, and mourned that she would never be able to eat it again. Often she prepared a meal just to look at it, smell it. I could no longer enjoy food. A bite of ice cream reminded me of my mother's suffering and deprivation. I lost ten pounds.

Some days she chatted lightly about her funeral. "What are we going to do with me? My hair? I can wear my fake diamonds. I want to look pretty when I'm in the coffin." Horrified, Danielle or I would ask her to stop. "I want to make everything a breeze—why not? What else have I got to do here? I've got time to plan; I'm lucky. It's very fashionable now, to plan your own funeral. Everybody's doing it. What some people do is take a hotel room to sit shivah. I like pale flowers—white, some pink—English country flowers, mostly roses. No big, horsey flowers, no lilies."

As August wore on, her physical appearance grew startling. Each week she seemed to age a decade. It was impossible to reconcile my young, beautiful mother with the sick old woman she had become. She was all bones except for a distended stomach that looked like it belonged to a starving Ethiopian child. Her posture was stooped. She didn't wear wigs at home, and what was left of her hair was thin and gray. In addition, she was increasingly incoherent. Some days her slurred words were indiscernible. She shuffled through the house restlessly and had to be watched like an infant. But her personality continued to shine through. She hated being watched. Just when we thought she was helpless, she would surprise us. A shipment of dishes arrived for a customer and she insisted on individually wrapping each dish in bubble wrap for delivery. She finished in lightning speed, and looked up at us triumphantly.

Her connection to the physical world never waned. One day, UPS delivered a package full of clothing she had ordered. The hospice nurse, Sharon, was there when my mom opened the box. She asked Sharon how much longer she had to live. Sharon was a compassionate woman, but she was always straight: "Maybe a week or two." My mother flew into a panic. "I have to return the sweaters!" Sharon tried to calm her, saying the sweaters were not important, her girls would deal with it, but my mother would not rest until it was done.

My mother loved to lie on the sofa in the enclosed porch that looked out over the backyard with the flower gardens and the white picket fence. I sat with her there one warm summer afternoon, her feet on my lap. She said, "If I get better, I'm going to do charity work, help others who are sick. If I don't get better, will you do it for me?" I said of course I would. I reminded her that she always used to talk about volunteering with animals, particularly dogs. "Dogs are nice, but I want to help people. You have no idea what it's like, what it means, to have everyone caring for me like this. I can't describe it." Her hazel eyes were full of emotion and awe. I was deeply moved by this. It took metastasized cancer at the age of sixty for my mother to grasp fully what it meant to nurture and be nurtured.

My mother worried out loud about what would happen to me

and Danielle after she was gone. She loved Bruce and enacted the classic deathbed scene of begging Danielle to marry him as her final wish, adding a quick postscript: "But no pressure." She made Bruce promise that he would always watch out for her girls. Danielle and I would sit by her bed and she'd say to us, "I love you, and I love you, and I love you, both the same. I love you more than my life."

Some days she drifted in and out of consciousness, falling asleep standing up at the table, sitting on the toilet. She used Compazine suppositories for nausea and could no longer manage them herself. Danielle and I put on rubber gloves and inserted them for her. In my nightmares, I could never have conjured the horror of my fastidious mother in this state with myself as her nurse.

Our mother's body was ready to go, but she continued to fight like a wildcat, Sharon said, which was only going to extend and increase her suffering, so she recommended that my sister and I assure our mother that it was all right to let go, that she didn't need to worry about us. We followed instructions, but it did not loosen our mother's grip.

One day I repeated gently, "You don't have to hold on anymore, Mom. We'll always love you, we'll think about you every day. But we will be okay. You're going to go to a better place."

She gave a skeptical raise of her eyebrow and replied in her slurred voice: "There is no better place."

Sharon and other hospice nurses told us that often the patient decides for herself when it's time to pass away. One day my mother demanded that Danielle and I summon our father and Bruce over immediately. "I'm very close," she said. "This is it." She lay down on the bed, all of us huddling around her, sobbing and telling her we loved her. At the end of this wrenching scene, she sat up and said, "Actually, I'm not going to go now. I'm going to go in the night. Tomorrow, when you wake up, I'll be gone." Our vigil was put on hold for a couple of hours and then resumed that evening. One of my mother's dearest friends came over to join us in our good-bye, but it had the effect of making my mom chatty. She invited her friend for dinner the next day: "We'll order in, make a fire in the living room. . . ." Danielle had staked out a place on an air mattress next to my mother's bed and refused to budge. "This is the end—the nurses said she could pick when to leave, and she chose tonight," she said, tears pouring down her face.

"I know," I said, "but I think she forgot."

One morning in September, my mother woke up with a stunning burst of energy. She was loopy when she called Bruce: "We miss you we miss you we miss you now. What can we do today? Maybe we can go for a ride?" He came right over. She could no longer walk, so he carried her to the car. She wore her baseball cap with the ponytail and her dragon shirt. Danielle, Bruce, my mother, Jolie, and I went on a shopping spree at the outlet stores in Riverhead. She was ecstatic. "Pearls and cashmere! And bargains!" We planted her in a chair and Danielle brought over piles of clothes for her to try. She separated the good from the bad, spouting her expertise. She tried on an oversized purple top hat and posed for a picture. She kissed and hugged us, full of joy. That was her last good day.

My father had repeatedly asked my mother to remarry him. She always stubbornly refused—she was proud of the independent spirit that led her to choose divorce after thirty-five years of marriage. Yet—license or no license—my parents were family, and they both knew it. Whenever my dad proposed, she would joke that a psychic once told her she'd marry twice, and if she *did* decide to remarry him the prophesy would come true. Out of the blue one day, my mother said okay.

"Okay what?" my dad asked.

"I'll marry you," she said in her slurred speech.

An old friend of my father's—a judge—drove to the house on a sunny afternoon. We all gathered outside on the enclosed porch. My mother sat between me and my father on the wicker sofa, Dani and Bruce sat on a loveseat nearby, and the judge sat facing my parents in an armchair. My mother wore a lavender cowl-neck cashmere sweater that we'd purchased on our shopping spree at the outlets. When my parents said their vows, my mother was very woozy, and could stay awake for only minutes at a time. Whenever she came to, she reflexively uttered Danielle's name or mine.

One morning she lay comatose, her face drawn and wan, stomach bloated, white shock of hair frazzled as if scorched, head straight back on the pillow, mouth agape. Sharon looked at her with empathy and shook her head. My mother was unrecognizable. Yet every moment she was lucid, she mightily resisted death. Two things had become clear: She would never let go while she was in her beloved house, and she would never let go while her girls were by her side.

NINE

September 2003

Part of the hospice agreement was that my mother would die at home. There was no reason for her ever to go to a hospital again because there would be no resuscitation.

Danielle and I were traumatized by what was happening. Despite the months we spent by her side, watching her condition deteriorate, we were not emotionally prepared to be home alone with our mother at the moment of her death. We were saved by an act of nature. A terrible storm was coming and an electrical blackout was anticipated. The hospice nurses were afraid they would be unable to make it up the hill in the storm, so they arranged for my mother to be transferred to Southampton Hospital.

The wind howled as Bruce carried my mother to the car. She was wrapped in cashmere blankets and reclined in the front seat while Danielle, Jolie, and I climbed into the back. As we drove away, my mother stared out the window, touching her fingertips to the glass, and said, "Good-bye, sweet house."

Our dad and Sharon met us at the hospital. We took the elevator upstairs and checked in at the desk. The young nurses were daffy and clueless; they seemed more like stewardesses. "What is the reason for hospitalization?"

"End-state anxiety," Sharon answered.

We had requested a private room and were led to one on the maternity floor. In the hallway, you could hear the happy cries of babies, of lives just beginning.

By some stroke of luck, we had been assigned the VIP room. It was furnished like an elegant hotel suite. Soft light shone through sconces on dimmers; there was a green leather armchair, a pretty sofa with a fold-out bed. Sharon exclaimed, "How Stephanie Queller is this?"

We settled Mom into the bed, exchanging the hospital blanket for her own silky sage green quilt. Before she drifted out of consciousness, she whispered to Sharon, "I don't want to die."

The next morning, she fought to stay awake. Her appearance was frightening. Her face was gaunt, ashen, shriveled. Outside, the storm was raging. Sharon sent for Mary the pastor. Apparently, Mary had a knack for soothing dying patients, gently convincing them that it was okay to let go. Mary arrived, held my mother's hand, and quietly read to her from the Bible. Psalm 98, The Lord Works Miracles; Psalm 18, David's Song of Victory.

"And my cry came before Him, even into His Ears. He sent from above, He took me, He drew me out of many waters. . . ."

After an hour of listening to Mary's gentle voice and talk of faith, my mother said, "If it's fightable, I'm fightable."

Reinforcements were called in. The female cantor from our synagogue arrived. Our family had been attending High Holy Day services in East Hampton for over twenty years, and the cantor's voice was haunting, beautiful, and familiar. After seeing the cantor,

Sharon was certain our mother would let go. The cantor arrived, stroked her hair, sang the Sh'ma and another song about residing in the House of God. Mom was so happy to see her, she cried as the cantor sang, but when she left, my mother immediately struggled to get out of the bed. She called over her private nurse, Deloris, to help. "Must keep walking."

Danielle and I left the room to get sandwiches and bring them back upstairs. When we returned ten minutes later, our mother was hysterical; Sharon, Deloris, and Jolie were trying to calm her. She was afraid we wouldn't come back in time. Through her sobs she said, "I can't talk."

"It's okay, Mom," we said. "You don't have to talk."

"But I want to. I love you first, you second, you second, you first. I love you both equally."

Sharon took us aside and said, once again, that our mother was simply not going to let go in our presence. Danielle and I told her that we had no intention of leaving her side.

The following day, September 20, 2003, my mother's lungs filled with fluid. Every breath she took was like drowning. The thick, heavy, gurgling sound of her gasping breaths will forever haunt me. My mother's eyes were filled with terror, her mouth frozen in a permanent O. She refused to get near the bed—she equated the bed with death—and insisted on walking. Deloris was a large, strong woman. She held my mother up in her arms and walked, as if dancing with her. My father looked on, helpless and aghast. "She doesn't deserve this," he said. "My bride was stunning. So beautiful."

The last words of my mother's I could understand were "Help," and "This is against my will."

The doctor came and ordered shots of morphine to keep her sedated until she died.

We sat with her for hours while she slept. Danielle and I were shaking from trauma. It had stopped raining, and Bruce insisted we take a walk with him. We left our mother with Dad, Deloris, and Jolie. We walked the few blocks to the ocean. I stood still, staring at its vastness, my feet in the sand, while Danielle and Bruce waited for me on the road. Danielle called me to come on, and we headed back. We had been gone a total of twenty minutes. Bruce's cell phone rang. It was my father.

"It's over."

Danielle fell to her knees in the middle of the street.

I dropped beside her.

TEN

September 2004

hung up with the doctor from the cancer medical lab, my head spinning from the news of my "genetic mutation," and ran across the courtyard to the *Gilmore Girls* writers' room, where the rest of the staff had already gathered. This was not a simple task, as I was wearing high heels. I had inherited my mother's vast designer shoe collection because my sister's foot was a size too big. When my mother had been alive, I'd criticized her devotion to high fashion, my reproach extending to her sixty-some pairs of Manolos, Jimmy Choos, and Chanel stilettos. As her illness progressed and she became increasingly present as a mother, my judgments against the material things she loved were silenced. Now, every item that belonged to my mom was endowed with emotion, special because it had been hers. I'd begun wearing her heels to work. As I traipsed up the stairs to join the other writers, I realized I was literally and metaphorically walking in my mother's shoes.

I did my best to maintain my composure in the writers' room.

The doctor's statistics whizzed around in my head while I made up pitches on the fly: Lorelai spends her first night at Luke's and is caught in her underwear by Kirk . . . ? Caught shimmying down the trellis by Miss Patty and her band of child ballerinas . . . ?

On our break, I pulled Rebecca aside and told her, laughing and crying in disbelief, that I'd tested positive for the breast cancer gene. She burst into tears—only after which she asked, "What does that mean exactly?" I replied that a doctor with the world's worst bedside manner had just spewed statistics at me, but I confessed that I didn't really know what it meant, either.

There are proper channels to go through if one elects to undergo genetic testing. There are cancer prevention centers staffed with genetic counselors, armed with pamphlets, and offering spots in support groups. The sensible choice would have been to go to one of them for counseling and education before taking the test, but I chose not to. I opted to take the test at a lab where they had me sign a release form and then drew my blood, no questions asked. I was so convinced I would test negative that I didn't feel I had to bother with any of those steps.

After my conversation with Leslie Rosen several years earlier, when I'd first heard about the BRCA test, I made a mental note to take it at some point. I felt no urgency to do so—not one doctor had ever suggested I take it. My mother had never been tested; she died without knowing that such a test existed. There was no prior history of cancer in our family. My mom had believed her cancer was due to twenty-five years of a high-stress career in the garment center, and this explanation rang true to me. I knew that only one in ten cases of breast cancer was genetic. I also knew that if my mother had carried the mutation—which I felt was highly unlikely—I'd only have a 50 percent chance of inheriting it from her. I was absolutely certain I did *not* have the breast cancer gene.

I wanted to take the test simply for the peace of mind of having a clean bill of health in writing. I likened it to taking an HIV test every ten years or so—of course I knew I didn't have AIDS, but it was always comforting to see it in black and white. In spite of the fact that my mother had cancer twice, I did not feel the disease would ever strike *me*. I had witnessed the horror of cancer up close. I knew my mother had been shocked each time she'd been seized by cancer. And yet, strangely, I still felt invincible.

EIGHT WEEKS after my mother's death, my sister and I moved back into her house. It was the end of November, and Southampton was cold and quiet. The summer crowds had long since vacated; only the locals and the die-hards who made weekend trips year-round remained. The flowering trees along her driveway were now bare. Danielle and I wandered the halls of her beloved house like ghosts. It didn't feel real that we were there and she was not.

Since she had every intention of beating her cancer, my mother hadn't wrapped up her affairs. Her Southampton store remained full of antique dishes, crystal, and silver. Danielle and I decided the most practical solution would be to have a going-out-of-business sale and work in the shop ourselves. Bruce and our father helped. I had never understood the big fuss over china. "They're just *dishes*," I would say. It took less than a week of handling the delicate items my mother had hand-picked on shopping sprees across the country and in Europe for me to recognize they were treasures. In no time, I found myself hoarding things. "These are rare Limoges—we can't just give them away!" We kept a photo of Mom in a silver frame on the counter next to a candle that was always lit. Her customers poured in, asking, "Where's Stephanie?"

All were shocked at the news; many wept. My mother had kept her illness a secret. "She was so young," they would say, "so vibrant." Each customer had a personal story or memory about her to share. She'd given a silver rattle to one woman's grandchild; she'd comforted another woman through her divorce. All admired her exquisite taste. All described her happily fluttering around the shop like a hummingbird. Working among her precious things, sitting behind her counter, and listening to her customers' stories was a poignant way for me and Danielle to inhabit her life one last time.

We worked in the store all winter, finally closing up shop in early March. In May, I moved back to California to resume my own life. I got a job writing for *Gilmore Girls,* moved into a new apartment, and began catching up on mundane tasks I'd been long neglecting, like renewing my license at the DMV and getting my teeth cleaned. It was in that casual vein that I added taking the BRCA test to my list. I called my cousin, a doctor, and asked him to set up an appointment for me at a cancer lab. When nearly two months had passed and I still hadn't received the results, I was annoyed but considered it a good sign. Doctors call right away with bad news and tend not to bother when everything's fine.

Now, a year after my mother's death, Rebecca and I stood in the patch of grass behind the *Gilmore Girls* writers' building. She hugged me and held my hand, and we cried for a few minutes like children who knew something scary had happened but couldn't comprehend quite what. I kept repeating how shocked I was that I had tested positive. I'd never entertained it as a possibility. Rebecca tucked her long blond hair behind her ears, grabbed both my hands, and gazed at me intently with watery blue eyes. "Don't worry about this," she said with maternal compassion. "We'll learn more about it, we'll figure it out together. I will be right by your side." I knew she would, and it made me feel a little better. "Now, until we get further information, I think you should try and let it go."

And that's just what I did.

We kept our reservations that night at the Edendale, a hip restaurant in Los Feliz. After an hour of hanging out with friends and drinking cheap red wine, I'd forgotten all about the BRCA mutation. Over the next week, I casually informed a handful of my closest friends: "It's primarily an Ashkenazi Jewish gene—as if the Jews didn't already have enough problems. . . ." I had a very hazy, limited understanding of what the breast cancer gene was, and I did not seek out further information. I decided not to worry about it. I rationalized that since my mother got breast cancer when she was fifty-two and I was only thirty-four, I wouldn't need to think about it for at least another ten years. When people expressed concern, I pretended I knew what I was talking about and said, "It's no big deal—all it means is that I'll go for extra screening." After three years of tragedy and sadness, I had only recently been laughing again, enjoying dinners with friends, movies, hikes through the Hollywood Hills. I relished this return to freedom, so I pulled a Scarlett O'Hara: "I can't think about this right now. I'll think about it tomorrow."

The one exception to my willful oblivion was the day the lab results arrived in the mail. I had asked the doctor over the phone to send me a copy. It was a single sheet of paper headed by a futuristic logo beneath which read MYRIAD. I would later learn that Myriad Labs in Salt Lake City owns the patent for the BRCA test and thus processes all BRCA results, regardless of where in the country you give blood. To the left of the logo was stamped CONFIDENTIAL. This added to the outlaw feeling of the test. The fact that advances in biotechnology now made it possible to predict future illness from a blood sample already made me feel like I was living in a chilly, genetically predestined future. In the center of the report, POSITIVE FOR A DELETERIOUS MUTATION was printed in bold letters and framed by a rectangular box for emphasis. The paragraph underneath contained the grim statistics the doctor had told me over the phone, but in greater detail: "Deleterious mutations in BRCA1 may confer as much as an 87% risk of breast cancer and a 44% risk of ovarian cancer by age 70 in women. Mutations in BRCA1 have been reported to confer a 20% risk of a second breast cancer within five years of the first as well as a ten-fold increase in the risk of subsequent ovarian cancer."

I felt an ominous chill run through me. I was grateful that my mother had never known anything about this test. She had not had to suffer from the knowledge that she had passed this horrible genetic predilection on to me.

I read the report once, tucked it back into the envelope, put it in a drawer.

Then I blocked it out for three months.

ELEVEN

When I next opened the drawer, it was almost Christmas.

Throughout the fall, Rebecca and I had many great adventures. At work, we'd "borrow" the golf cart and drive wildly around the lot in our floppy sun hats and shades. We'd zoom off to the set or to the Warner Bros. gift shop to buy silly items that made us laugh——one afternoon we returned to the writers' room wearing matching yellow Tweety Bird T-shirts that read NATURAL BLONDE. I was dating and would invite the guy-of-the-week to the commissary for lunch so Rebecca could check him out. The three of us would sit at a sunny outdoor table with a view of New York Street and get tipsy on Chardonnay in the middle of the workday. Then we'd bid him good-bye and Rebecca and I would link arms, stroll through the make-believe town of Stars Hollow, giggling and debriefing, and more often than not tear the poor guy apart. We'd declare him a dud, or at least not nearly smashing enough, and decide to "send him back." On the weekends I spent a lot of time with Rebecca and her then-boyfriend, David. Their Los Feliz apartment was a den of creativity—they were both writers, but Rebecca was also an artist and photographer, and David expertly played the banjo. On a whim, they'd hung a thick piece of rope with knots from the living room ceiling and one of us was always climbing or swinging on it. We rarely mentioned the breast cancer gene, and for those three months it had not the slightest impact on my life.

By December, a nagging internal voice pushed through my carefree veneer and urged me to set up an appointment at a reputable clinic for preventing women's cancers—the sort of place I'd opted *not* to go for the BRCA test. I'd turned thirty-five in November and had never even had a mammogram. Though I'd convinced myself that my BRCA status would be of no real concern until I was around forty-five, I still understood that I needed regular screening. At this particular clinic I'd be able to take all the requisite tests in a single afternoon, rather than driving to different offices over the course of a week. I fished around in the drawer for my BRCA lab results because I'd been told to bring them to my appointment.

Rebecca and several other friends offered to go with me, but I said there was no need. I'd be taking a battery of routine tests. I expected the day to be simple and unremarkable. The woman had told me over the phone that they'd give me a fluffy white robe and slippers and I'd putter around the clinic going from mammogram to MRI to sonogram. It sounded almost spalike. I insisted it was no big deal—I'd be fine on my own.

I had the directions scribbled down on a scrap of paper and when I pulled up to the correct address, I was surprised to see that the clinic was located inside the hospital's cancer center. As I made a left into the underground parking structure, I saw a woman with a scarf partially concealing her bald head entering the building. It hadn't occurred to me that the clinic would be part of a real cancer center with real cancer patients.

I entered through the automatic doors and asked an official-looking person where the clinic was.

"Do you have a cancer center ID card?" she asked.

"No—I'm just here for the clinic. . . ."

She pointed to a desk to my left. "You need to get an ID card first. They'll tell you what to do next."

I got on line behind the bald woman in the scarf.

After filling out forms and becoming a card-carrying member of the cancer center, I was instructed to sit in the waiting area until someone from the clinic came out to get me.

A few minutes later, a woman with a blunt, preppy haircut appeared and headed in my direction. She wore a polka-dotted blouse tucked into a pencil skirt. When she greeted me, her expression was set into the pained smile of someone paying a condolence call. I assumed she was aware that my mother had recently died. "Jessica? Hi, I'm Cheryl." She held my hand for a beat too long, her voice thick with sympathy. "Follow me." She led me down the hall.

"Is this where I change into the robe for the tests?"

"No, I thought we would talk first," she replied. "I'm your genetic counselor."

She opened the door to a private room that was furnished with a small sofa and two armchairs. She took a seat in a chair, handed me a stack of papers, and indicated that I should sit in the chair across from her. One of the handouts was an expensively printed pamphlet on testing positive for BRCA and its statistical implications. Another handout was titled "Genetic Discrimination."

Cheryl's eyes focused on me like twin pools of pity.

"I usually meet women before they've taken the test, but you already know your BRCA status. Testing positive for the BRCA-1 mutation means you have up to an eighty-seven percent lifetime chance of getting breast cancer. How does that make you feel?"

All at once I understood that Cheryl's sympathy wasn't for the loss of my mother; it was for *me*. Rage surged, flushing my cheeks. I tried to calm down by focusing on the polka dots.

"Not thrilled," I replied to her question.

"You also have up to a forty-four percent lifetime chance of getting ovarian cancer, whereas a woman in the general population has a two percent chance. How does that make you feel?"

Was this woman kidding?

"My mother just died of ovarian cancer, how do you think it makes me feel?"

I crossed my arms, aware of my defensive posture.

"I'm sorry about your mother. Didn't I read in your chart that she also had breast cancer?"

"Yes."

"How old was she when she was diagnosed?"

"Fifty-two."

Cheryl seemed surprised by this answer.

"Fifty-two? That's late. She was lucky."

My mother was *lucky* to have gotten cancer at fifty-two? Now I was outraged.

"Most women tell me their lives are split in half—life before they found out they carried the BRCA genetic mutation and life after. They say nothing was ever the same again."

I stared at her, speechless and seething.

"Those white pages outline your legal rights in the event that a health insurance company denies you coverage on the basis of genetic discrimination. The Americans with Disabilities Act prohibits genetic discrimination in the workplace and in group insurance policies, and so far there have been no reported cases. But we're looking for a case of discrimination to serve as a prototype, so if you experience this, let us know. I see you're all set up for thorough screening today, including your first mammogram. Those can be scary tests. How do you feel?"

"I *feel* like you're treating me as if cancer is imminent. I just turned thirty-five—my mother didn't get breast cancer until she was fifty-two. I thought this was something I'd have to be concerned about ten years down the line. Are you telling me I need to be worried *now*?"

Cheryl seemed oblivious to my hostility and disbelief.

"Well, you'll see in the pamphlet that statistically you have a fifty percent chance of getting breast cancer before the age of fifty. . . . BRCA mutations are known for causing early-onset cancer."

Then the zinger:

"At some point you may want to consider chemoprevention or prophylactic surgery, like mastectomy or oophorectomy."

I was shaking when I left the session with Cheryl. I was not sad or afraid—I was indignant. How dare she smile and spew out those horrible statistics? And scare me with chemoprevention and prophylactic surgery? Mastectomy? Was she out of her mind? And how dare she make me feel like I was in some kind of danger? That was supposed to be therapeutic?

I entered the inner sanctum of the clinic, put on a plush white robe, and went through the round of tests, the experience anything but spalike. Squooshing my boobs down onto the metal lever of the mammogram machine was a cold, clinical event. The MRI machine was claustrophobic, loud, and eerie. Giving blood for the CA-125 ovarian cancer test chilled me to the core. It was the test my mother had taken with trepidation every week of her illness, the test that had accurately predicted her demise. After physical exams with a gynecologist and oncologist, I had my final test—a breast sonogram. Two doctors huddled around the screen, whispering—never a good sign. The sonogram, they told me, showed a cyst of some sort. They said that my large breasts were dense and naturally cystic, which would prove to be an obstacle to cancer screening. I would always have "areas of nodularity" like the one in question. These areas would usually be harmless, but because of my genetic status, I would have to be extremely cautious. They told me to come back in a few weeks to check if the cyst had gone away on its own; if it hadn't, we'd do a needle biopsy. The lady at the desk took my robe and scheduled my next appointment.

I sobbed the entire drive home.

Once in my apartment, I vented to Rebecca over the phone, chronicling every odious detail of the day. I said I'd go back to get the cyst checked, but I vowed *never* to subject myself to Cheryl or genetic counseling again. She agreed that it all sounded dreadful. After airing my grievances to Rebecca, I felt as if I had more anger and hurt to purge, so I called my friend Kay in New York.

Kay had been my freshman roommate and had remained one of my closest friends ever since. We had been inseparable in college and were an odd pair: a theatrical little Jewish girl from Bleecker Street who acted in plays and listened to Stephen Sondheim and a tall, striking, intellectual black girl with a blunt personality from Jackson, Mississippi. We'd both grown up to be writers—I wrote teleplays, while she was a journalist covering international affairs. We spoke on the phone almost every night.

I dialed Kay and launched into a rant. I reenacted the scene with Cheryl, expressing outrage at the insufferable treatment I felt I'd endured. "Can you believe she actually suggested a *mastectomy*? She treated me like I was already a cancer patient!" Kay was not one to mince words, but I noticed that she was unusually silent.

The next day Kay called back, and with her sister Erika chiming in in the background, she ambushed me. She said that after I'd tested positive she'd had a bad feeling about how nonchalant I was acting, so she did some research of her own. She was disturbed by what she'd learned. To investigate further, she called Erika's old Harvard friend Kim, a breast surgeon. Kim told Kay that as soon as someone tests positive for a BRCA mutation, she *is* treated like a cancer patient. Kim also said that the most common reaction of women who test positive is to play ostrich. Kay insisted that's just what I'd done—I'd burrowed my head in the sand so deeply that when a certified genetic counselor presented the facts, I responded with indignation. She went on to say that Kim the breast surgeon saw cases of deadly cancer every day and felt it was essential for me to get a bilateral mastectomy as soon as possible. But not to worry—plastic surgery could do marvels these days—I could pick out a lovely new pair of breasts.

I balked at Kay's intervention and told her to back off. As Kay well knew, I was single and wanted to find a partner and have children. Was she out of her mind? There was no way I was going to *cut my breasts off*. Kay stayed committed to her bossiness. She insisted that cancer—as *I* well knew—was not something to mess with. "You need to have this operation because I love you and do not want you to die."

I hung up in a huff, deeply rattled.

I hadn't told Kay about the cyst that my breast sonogram

had revealed. Or that I had to go back to the clinic for a possible needle biopsy. I sank into the white sofa in my airy new
Beachwood Canyon apartment. I'd recently moved in and, like
the job on *Gilmore Girls,* the apartment was a symbol of my fresh
start. My mother's illness, death, and those excruciating months of
mourning were all finally behind me. This was supposed to be my
return to dinner parties and dating and—at worst—wallowing in
sweatpants over a guy who hadn't called me back, watching *Annie
Hall* for solace. This new genetic predicament was some kind of
perverse joke.

I thought about how cavalierly I'd taken the BRCA test. How
certain I was that I would test negative. In perfect hindsight, I
understood the value of seeing a genetic counselor *before* taking
the test. I hadn't bothered to be apprised of what I was getting
myself into. I'd given no thought to whether this was information
I actually wanted. My mind kept returning to the fact that my
mom hadn't been diagnosed with breast cancer until age fifty-two.
Surely that meant I had some more time. Maybe I should have
waited, say, until forty-five to take the test; that would have given
me a decade of blissful ignorance in which to fall in love, have
kids, breast-feed. . . .

My hand instinctively went to my right breast, trying to feel
the cyst in question. The night before, I had searched for it with
such intensity that I'd pinched myself black-and-blue. I couldn't
really feel a lump—but neither could my mother feel her small
tumor when she'd been diagnosed with advanced breast cancer. I
suddenly remembered that Kay's friend Sarah had just lost a childhood friend, our age, to breast cancer, though Kay had refrained
from bringing that up.

I had a flash of how my mother had raised me to be her

"clone," and of how hard I'd worked to differentiate myself from her. The ultimate irony: Regardless of my efforts, I was genetically programmed to be just like my mother or at least to meet the same terrible fate. I felt a heaviness in my chest. I closed my eyes and followed my breath for a few moments like I used to when I practiced meditation. Beneath the heaviness, the emotion I identified was dread.

WHEN I PULLED UP to the cancer center several weeks later, my sister sat in the passenger seat beside me. Danielle was living in Los Angeles for the winter and had insisted on coming along to hear what the doctor had to say about my cyst. After what we'd been through, we were both spooked by the mere suggestion of cancer. However, Danielle had not taken the BRCA test and adamantly declared she never would. She felt that living with the knowledge that she had the breast cancer gene would be oppressive. It was bad enough, she said, that she'd now constantly have to worry about me.

I'd been so overwhelmed by all the new information during my first visit to the clinic that I'd drifted through the tests in a daze. This time, I was charged up—ready to take matters into my own hands aggressively, just like my medical malpractice attorney father had trained me to do.

When I entered the exam room, rather than lying on the table, I marched up to the radiologist in my fluffy white robe, my sister in tow, and demanded that the cyst be biopsied. Dr. Parker was kind and good-natured. He laughed and said, "Let's see if there's anything there, first, shall we?" When I opened my robe he was startled by the black-and-blue marks on my right breast.

I admitted sheepishly, "I've been trying to feel the cyst."

"You're not even in the right area," he replied.

He found the cyst on the sonogram but said it had grown smaller and was certainly not cancer. I was too wound up in Attorney-Fred-Queller's-daughter mode to let it go at that.

"I want you to biopsy it anyway."

"I agree," Danielle chimed in.

"It's all the way against the chest wall; a needle biopsy would be difficult and is utterly unnecessary."

"I'm not going to have peace of mind unless you perform a biopsy," I replied.

"All I do every day is look for and identify breast cancer, Jessica. I assure you this is not it."

Dr. Parker suggested that we talk in his office and he'd answer as many of our questions about the BRCA mutation as he could. At the very least, he wanted to calm me down so that I wouldn't pinch myself black-and blue-again.

With my sister beside me, I sat across from the doctor in my white terry-cloth robe; I still had to be examined by the clinic's oncologist before I was free to go. I crossed my arms and furrowed my brow, intent on assuming control of the situation. I wanted Dr. Parker to see me as a force to be reckoned with; I had no awareness that I must have looked like a disgruntled lady at Burke Williams Day Spa, huffing because the sauna was broken. He repeated the BRCA-1 statistics that I already knew by heart: up to an 87 percent lifetime chance of breast cancer, up to a 44 percent lifetime chance of ovarian. Current studies showed that chemoprevention, like tamoxifen, had proved effective only for women who were BRCA-2-positive. The doctor explained that women with the BRCA-1 mutation had only two choices, each of which had major drawbacks: to undergo increased cancer surveillance, or to have prophylactic surgery. The first, obviously, was the conservative approach; to watch and wait and hope for the best. The second, more radical option—to remove breasts or ovaries in a preemptive strike—was the most effective protection from cancer, but a hard decision for most women to make.

Hard decision? Deciding whether to go to law school or take one's chances as a writer is a hard decision. Deciding whether to have amniocentesis when you're pregnant is a hard decision. Deciding to cut off your breasts when you don't have cancer and possibly never will? To me, that was insanity. At the same time, passively waiting for cancer to strike, relying on inexact surveillance machines, hoping to catch it before it spread—that didn't sound reasonable, either.

"What do doctors recommend to women in my position? What's the protocol?"

"Well . . . unfortunately, doctors can't yet offer any definitive guidance. The BRCA test has only been in existence for about nine years. It's a case of science outpacing our ability to know what to do with the data."

"You're telling me you don't know how to advise me?"

"I'm going to a seminar on this topic next month. I'll be happy to e-mail you anything I learn. . . ."

Danielle and I gazed at him in disbelief. If doctors were at a loss on this subject, how could a patient be expected to make the best decision?

Across the hall, a few minutes later, the oncologist gave me a quick follow-up physical exam. He was in his fifties, a man of few words. He shook his head at the black-and-blue marks I'd inflicted on myself.

"I've been a little nervous," I offered.

Though I knew I would never consider removing my breasts, I asked the doctor for his opinion. He confirmed what Dr. Parker had said—there was no clear course of action. I said I found it mind-boggling that the experts had no advice for women in my position. Then I asked the age-old question posed to doctors: "What would you tell me to do if I were your daughter or your wife?" The doctor took his time, was thoughtful with his answer. He replied that prophylactic bilateral mastectomy was the "gold standard" for preventing breast cancer in BRCA-positive women, and that he would strongly advocate it for a woman who was married and had finished bearing children. But for someone like me, who was single and whose personal life was not yet settled—he couldn't recommend it in good conscience.

"Having your breasts removed doesn't interfere with having children, does it?" I asked.

"No . . . but it affects delicate issues of sexuality, body image, intimacy. . . . For a young woman who's dating, there's no telling what kind of adverse affect it might have. . . ."

This doctor, this man, was compassionate and sincerely grappling with what would be in my best interests. Though he did not spell it out, his concern was loud and clear: I was a young woman who wanted to have a family. Removing my breasts might prevent cancer, but might it also prevent a man from finding me attractive or marrying me . . . ?

Danielle and I left the clinic exhausted, but I had a clean bill of health. I told Danielle I was not even going to *think* about this subject for a year, maybe two.

KAY AND I had spoken several times since her intervention, but we'd skirted around the volatile issue. A few days after my second clinic visit, she called me with a question:

"How would you like to write an Op-Ed piece about having a BRCA mutation?"

Though Kay was a freelance writer, she was currently working as an editor for the Op-Ed page of the *New York Times*. I'd grown up watching my father read the *Times* every morning before heading to court to argue a case. I revered the *New York Times*. She might as well have asked how I'd like to win a Pulitzer or bring about world peace.

"Really, Kay?" I asked.

"Nothing's guaranteed. All Op-Ed pieces are submitted on spec. But I pitched it to my boss, and he's interested."

I was planning on sticking my ostrich head back in the sand. But now that I had a prestigious writing assignment? I would learn everything there was to know about the BRCA gene.

I went online and began my research.

TWELVE

When I decided to quit acting and become a television writer, I had no idea whether I was actually capable of writing scripts. I had a notion I could do it. I was certainly better equipped to write scripts than I was to solve physics problems or fix cars. When the esteemed producer Ron Schwary offered me my first writing job—to adapt a novel into a screenplay—the only things I'd ever written were two sample TV episodes (one of which he'd read and liked). "You know how to adapt a book into a movie, don't you?" he asked.

"Of course," I replied with confidence.

Then I ran to Barnes & Noble in a panic and bought every book ever printed on the subject. I didn't know how to construct a screenplay, never mind adapt a novel. But I took the money and mustered my courage, resigned to sink or swim. Every significant accomplishment of my life has been achieved by this method. Writing an Op-Ed piece for the *New York Times* was no exception.

I had no idea if I could do it. I had no idea *how* to do it. But I was determined to act as if I did and see what happened.

For two months I came home directly after work, changed into sweats, tied my hair up in a ponytail, sat at my desk, and scoured the Internet for articles on the BRCA mutation. I drank cans of Diet Coke while guiltily thinking that I should be drinking green tea. (Chemicals: bad for cancer prevention; antioxidants: good.) Soon I was inundated with material. With each new piece of information I called my sister, Kay, Rebecca, or other close friends to fill them in on what I'd learned. I drove everyone crazy. I'd decided to become an expert on cancer and genetics, and my poor loyal comrades wearily held up their side of the call as I spouted. I was educating myself in order to convince myself that I could write an Op-Ed piece on the subject, yet as the mysteries of the BRCA genes unfolded, I grew increasingly emotional. There was no denying that this was not just an assignment. This was my life.

After skimming a handful of BRCA articles, I realized I ought to address a couple of fundamental questions. The first: What is cancer?

In simplest terms, according to Wikipedia: "Cancer is a class of diseases or disorders characterized by *uncontrolled divisions of cells* and the ability of these cells to spread, either by direct growth into adjacent tissue or through invasion, or by implantation into distant sites by metastasis."

That was clear enough. Next, I needed to revisit ninth-grade biology: What are genes?

The Lexicon encyloBio definition: "A gene is a sequence of DNA contained within the nucleus of our cells that carries the 'instructions' for the manufacture of a protein. The information they hold describes the myriad characteristics of an individual (e.g. eye color). Human beings have approximately 30,000 genes."

I learned that everyone has BRCA-1 and BRCA-2 genes. Only a small percentage of people wind up with a BRCA gene that is mutated. ("The Chosen People" ironically came to mind—as I'd discovered earlier, the highest incidence of BRCA mutations happens to be found among Ashkenazi Jews.) A breast surgeon explained genetic mutations to me in this way: "When we construct buildings, bridges, and tunnels, an error in the plan or blueprint, if not corrected, will result in a defective product. Similarly, a defect in a gene may lead to a defect in the corresponding protein. A mutation is a change in the DNA sequence or code, resulting in an altered protein structure. The structural change in protein, may, in turn, result in defective protein function."

The normal function of BRCA genes is to repair DNA and control cell division. When cells divide without normal control, they accumulate into a mass of extra tissue: a tumor. The BRCA genes are known as tumor suppressors. When BRCA genes are mutated— or defective—they may not be able to do their job properly.

I learned that BRCA mutations are rare—only a small percentage of people wind up with a BRCA gene that is defective. One estimate suggests that BRCA-1 mutations occur in about one out of every eight hundred people in the general population, while BRCA-2 mutations are even less frequent. BRCA mutations account for only 5 to 10 percent of all breast cancers diagnosed in America.

Another important concept that was explained to me by a surgeon is why BRCA expression is limited to certain parts of the body. All genes are present in all cells. Each gene is associated with several "off and on" switches that are activated or suppressed to different extents in different cell types. BRCA genes primarily affect tumor growth in breasts and ovaries.

Online, I investigated the differences between BRCA-1 and BRCA-2. Though the genes are similar in function, they are located on different chromosomes. This means that, when mutated, each gene carries a different degree of risk for breast and ovarian cancer. Most studies confirmed the BRCA-1 statistics I knew by heart: up to an 87 percent percent lifetime risk of breast cancer; up to a 44 percent lifetime risk of ovarian cancer. BRCA-2 mutations confer a lower risk of ovarian cancer (up to a 25 percent chance) and a higher risk of male breast cancer (6 percent chance). BRCA-2 mutations carry the same risk of female breast cancer as BRCA-1 mutations but a slightly lower risk of developing cancer in a second breast.

I learned a few other notable facts: If one parent carries a BRCA mutation, each of his or her offspring will have a 50 percent chance of inheriting it. Both BRCA mutations confer up to an 18 percent chance of prostate cancer. Prophylactic double mastectomy reduces a BRCA-positive woman's risk by around 90 percent, but not to zero. It is currently impossible to remove all breast tissue, as it is intimately associated with the overlying skin and tissue in the axillae (arm pits). Similarly, prophylactic oophorectomy reduces the risk of ovarian cancer, but also not to zero.

Once I had digested these central concepts, I eagerly turned to articles that related personal stories. The first one that knocked me out remains—to my mind—the best piece currently written on the subject: Dr. Jerome Groopman's superb essay "Decoding Destiny."

The essay appeared in the *New Yorker* and was later printed as a chapter in Groopman's book *Second Opinions*. It relays the story of his patient Karen Belz. Karen tested BRCA-2-positive at age thirty-four. Her mother had recently died from breast cancer. Her sister, Ruth—just two years older than Karen—had just been diagnosed with metastasized breast cancer at thirty-six. By the time Ruth's cancer was detected by a routine mammogram, it had already spread to her bones and lungs. All three women carried the same mutant gene. Karen went to see Dr. Groopman because she didn't want to be a sitting duck, waiting for cancer to strike. She turned to Groopman for advice about what action to take. Dr. Groopman acknowledges in the essay that he felt off balance as a doctor in this case. Just like my doctors at the cancer clinic in Los Angeles, he was unable to give Karen clear advice because the protocol wasn't yet determined. He presented her with the same two unsatisfactory choices I had been given: Submit to vigilant surveillance and hope for the best, or undergo radical surgery. There was no middle ground. Like me, Karen was horrified by having witnessed her mother's death (her horror now exacerbated by a sister with advanced cancer), yet equally horrified by the idea of removing her breasts and ovaries. She said she couldn't do it.

When Karen leaves the office, Groopman grapples with the anguish of genetic terrors. He writes: "Perhaps it was best for us all to remain ignorant, so that life could progress naturally, without the burden of deadly prophesies." The story ends with Karen returning to Groopman's office, having decided to remove her breasts and ovaries after all. Her husband wants her to do it and has assured her she will remain desirable to him. Her sister, Ruth, was the real deciding factor. Ruth was riddled with cancer and feared she wouldn't live to see her kids grow up. After soul-searching, Karen decides that she is lucky to have been given advance warning. Karen wants to do everything possible to prevent cancer and be around for her own children.

I was shaken by this essay. The logic of it was unassailable, but I did not want to face its conclusion.

Several points struck me. Though Karen had been thirty-four— a year younger than I was—she already had a husband who loved her and had given birth to children. This seemed a world away from my own situation. But this fact alarmed me: Karen and Ruth's mother had died at a relatively old age from breast cancer—why had Ruth developed aggressive cancer at thirty-six? I read the essay again carefully and focused on a specific line: *"One set of clinical data on BRCA mutations indicates that the age at which tumors first occur is highly variable."*

This sentence gave me knots in my stomach.

My defense was the fact that my mother had not been diagnosed with breast cancer until the age of fifty-two. I was clinging to the notion that this meant I would not likely develop cancer until around the same age. I was relying on the assumption that there was consistency in the age of cancer onset between BRCA-positive mothers and daughters, though I hadn't put this question to my doctors.

Next, I read an article in *People* magazine that threw me into a tizzy. There were five sisters in the Kimball family. Cindy developed breast cancer at thirty-one, which shocked them all. Next Kristi felt a lump, which also turned out to be cancer. Then Wendi followed. *Three sisters had all been diagnosed with breast cancer in their thirties.* A doctor at Duke University Medical Center suggested that the whole family take the BRCA test. All five sisters tested positive for BRCA-1, inherited from their father. The fourth sister, Tammy, was in her late thirties, married with children, and opted for prophylactic mastectomy and oophorectomy. Jennifer, the fifth sister, was thirty-four and newly married. She planned to undergo both surgeries directly after having children.

What was the deal with all these BRCA-positive women getting breast cancer in their thirties? My anxiety turned manic. I paced around the apartment with the phone, telling every friend who would listen about the Kimball sisters. This was not good. Not good at all.

The next article I read that had a strong impact on me was about a woman named Sue Friedman. Sue had never been considered at high risk for cancer, yet she was diagnosed with breast cancer at thirty-three. Later, Sue read an article about the BRCA test in a magazine. No doctor had ever mentioned it to her. She sought out the test and discovered she carried the BRCA-2 mutation. Sue subsequently had her breasts and ovaries removed at thirty-five. She looked for an online BRCA support group for women and could not find one, so she started her own—FORCE: Facing Our Risk of Cancer Empowered.

The FORCE Web site opened a whole new world to me. Dozens, maybe hundreds of BRCA-positive women congregated at this site. They called one another "sister" and spoke a language all their own. At first I was put off by the lingo—I was afraid I'd stumbled onto a cult. Women who carried a BRCA mutation but had never been diagnosed with cancer were called "previvors." These people spoke in a shorthand comprised of mysterious acronyms. After a while I could decipher some of them: PS translated to "plastic surgeon"; BSO was "bilateral salpingo-oophorectomy"; DH—maybe "dear husband" . . . ? I felt like a spy reading personal, foreign correspondence. The dialogue was startlingly intimate and frank. At the same time, there was a sugarcoating—an abundant use of smiley faces and hearts. Once I got past the trappings of the site, I recognized FORCE as a tremendous resource. The message board had threads posted on every imaginable aspect of the BRCA mutation experience. Many topics went into microscopic detail about mastectomy and reconstruction, ranging from the different types of procedures available to what to wear at the hospital. There were threads on drainage tubes, expanders, silicone implants, gummy bear implants, scars, incisions, nipple reconstruction. . . . The site went into the same kind of detail on oophorectomy, hysterectomy, hormone replacement therapy, and so on. The wealth of information was overwhelming—too much for me. I was not ready or willing to look at the actual components of prophylactic surgery.

I skimmed the message board for threads about other women in my position—young(ish), single, dating, desiring a family, and BRCA-positive. There were scads of women my age with the mutation, but little evidence of single women grappling with my particular issues. It seemed to be the only BRCA topic not exhaustively dissected.

And then I found a thread that addressed the dreaded question: Was there consistency in the age of cancer onset among family members with the same mutation? I was distraught to learn that the answer was no. Mothers and daughters and aunts with the same genetic variant often developed cancer at entirely different ages, while some never got it at all. There was no medical consensus on what factors caused expression of the gene. However, it was generally accepted that diet, reproductive patterns, and environmental exposure played roles. I found another link in which each woman posted the age at which her family members were diagnosed with cancer: A mother at seventy; her daughter at thirty-four. A grandmother at forty-one; her daughter at fifty-eight; her granddaughter at thirty.

My false sense of security evaporated, just like that. The fact that my mother was diagnosed with cancer at fifty-two had little bearing on when my cancer might surface.

My mind raced and my phone rants to friends reached a fever pitch. Studies showed that early pregnancy helped ward off breast cancer—my mother had had two babies in her twenties, but I was thirty-five with no kids. . . . On the other hand, late menarche was said to hold off breast cancer and I had been the last among my friends to get my period at fifteen, in the tenth grade. . . . Maybe I was exposed to worse environmental factors than my mother, living in the twenty-first century in smoggy Hollywood. Maybe I used the wrong deodorant. Maybe I didn't eat enough broccoli. . . .

I thought back to the genetic counselor, Cheryl, of whom I'd been so critical. I thought about how she'd expressed surprise that my mother hadn't gotten breast cancer until age fifty-two because BRCA mutations are known to cause "early-onset cancer": a 50 percent chance of getting breast cancer before the age of fifty. I'd had a 50 percent chance of inheriting the faulty gene from my mother in the first place. Before this experience, I'd been a "glass half full" kind of person and had considered 50 percent decent odds. Now that I'd landed on the wrong side of the coin toss, 50 percent held an entirely different meaning. If you're on the wrong side of 50 percent, it might as well be 100 percent. Suddenly 50 percent was a terrifying, ominous probability.

For the first time, I allowed myself to think about what it might mean to remove my breasts, to imagine the possibility.

This unpleasant reverie led to the vast subject of my relationship to my body.

Harriette, my mother, Danielle, and I all had similar builds: slim and stacked. In contrast to the other three women in my family, I'd always been ambivalent (at best) about having large breasts.

In her actress heyday, Harriette had treated her figure as a vital tool of her trade. She dressed like a sexpot and worked her Rita Hayworth curves for all they were worth. My mother was of the same "if you've got it, flaunt it" school. She taught me and my sister that the purpose of a woman's outfit was not to shelter her from the elements, but to show off her figure. My grandmother was a stunning Hollywood starlet, my mother a glamorous fashion designer. Both women passed on their wisdom to me and Danielle: Of all the attributes, beauty came first. And beauty to them was not just a pretty face; it meant being thin, leggy, and busty. At six, I'd be playing in the ocean with my little friend Lizzie while my mother watched us from the beach. When I got out of the water and ran to my mom to get a towel, she'd say: "Your legs are so much longer than Lizzie's! Her tush starts just above your knees. . . ." I must have been around eight—and flat as a board—when my mother first instructed me: "No matter how much money they offer you, never pose topless." The assumption of course was that I'd one day be a buxom beauty and sought after by Hugh Hefner. My mom repeated that edict many times over the years. Gradually she let details of the backstory slip: When she was twenty, some man in Vegas had offered her a small fortune to be his model, which she promptly turned down. Her mother, Harriette, had also refused several such offers.

I had never been comfortable with my oversexualized grandmother and mother. In my early twenties, I yearned to be valued for my intellect—or at least for some substantive reason like my interests or talents. To my mother's horror, I wore oversized sweaters and sacklike peasant dresses. I started therapy around that time (like any nice, upper-middle-class, neurotic New York Jewish girl), and Edith, my therapist, broached the topic in one of our first few sessions. Why did I wear only large, baggy clothes? I told her it was a feminist thing. I did not want a man to be interested in me because I was thin and large-breasted. If he liked me for the right reasons—and I elected to sleep with him—that would be a pleasant surprise. Edith was skeptical of my pat response and got me talking about my mom and Harriette. She concluded that I was repressing my own sexuality because of my critical feelings toward my mother. Why should I feel that I had to hide my body? she asked. I knew there was some validity to her theory. However, I made the case that I had a different ideal of beauty than my mother did—I was drawn to a more subtle and, in my opinion, more sophisticated aesthetic. For instance, I loved how dancers looked, the elegance of their carriage, their posture. I was petite with narrow shoulders and my bra size was a 32D. I always felt my breasts were too large for my frame and that emphasizing them in clothes looked cheap or gauche. I longed for smaller, dancer breasts, though I never considered the extreme measure of a breast reduction. Despite my ambivalence about my large breasts, all of my boyfriends had sung their praises. This was not lost on me. There was something I was cultivating that smacked of the librarian who takes her glasses off, lets her hair down, and is suddenly a sex goddess. I had an aversion to the overtly sexy look, but I enjoyed the drama of surprising new boyfriends behind closed doors.

Whatever my feelings on the matter, being a buxom Jewess was a large part of my identity. I played the role of Anne Frank when I was twenty-one at the Lyric Stage, a small theater in Boston. In the play, Anne ages from thirteen to fifteen. It is not uncommon for actresses in their early twenties to be cast as Anne. However, when Anne is thirteen in early scenes of the play, she jumps in her father's lap and clings to him in childish ways. I was a full-bodied woman—from that there was no escape. This led my review in the Boston *Phoenix* to read: "Alas, Queller's vixenish Anne Frank . . ." Large breasts had turned my earnest performance into a tawdry scene.

During my relationship with Adrian he would tease me by calling me "Skinny McBooby," which really annoyed me. I felt it was a stripper nickname (and considering that Adrian's first wife was a stripper named Cinnamon, it was little wonder that it appealed

to him). I had a bimbo complex from my Tiffany days—I strove
to be an intelligent, elegant, substantive woman. Skinny McBooby
did little to advance that image. Somewhere along the line I'd
started equating my big boobs with the bimbo persona I so loathed.
I had a love-hate relationship with my breasts. I did not want to
be valued for them. I did not like the effect of emphasizing them
in clothes. I strove for a more refined beauty. At the same time,
I understood that men found my body sexy and I liked that. As
long as I was appreciated for my mind, quirks, and sensibility *first,*
I had no problem with lovers admiring my body in private. Of
course I wanted them to. I looked down on my mom and Harriette for placing the highest premium on a desirable figure, but I
still internalized its value.

Wearing clothes that partially concealed my body was an act of
rebellion. But having a mastectomy? That was unthinkable. Underneath it all, I was Stephanie's daughter—I had been raised with the
notion that one day men would offer great sums of money for the
privilege of documenting my breasts. When she'd been told she
had breast cancer but wouldn't require a mastectomy, my mother
said, "Thank God"—she would be able to keep her beautiful
breasts intact.

But that had been before. Before any of us understood what
cancer was. At the end of her life, my mother—the devotee to
beauty—would have given up her breasts in a heartbeat. I knew
with absolute certainty that she would have done anything to live.

THIRTEEN

Once I allowed the real possibility of mastectomy to enter my consciousness, life as I knew it ended. This was what Cheryl-the-genetics-counselor must have meant when she said that most women who tested positive felt their lives had been split into "before" and "after." I stumbled around in a fog, brooding over my existential dilemma: "To cut my breasts off, or not to cut my breasts off, that is the question. . . ."

Something else weighed heavily on me: I hadn't yet told my father I'd taken a genetic test, never mind that I had the mutation. I'd been trying to think of a way to soften the blow. I decided that if I immediately followed "Dad, I have the breast cancer gene" with "I have an assignment to write an Op-Ed piece for the *New York Times!*" it might help, at least momentarily. My dad loved to kvell—his greatest pleasure was hearing of his kids' accomplishments and then recounting them to everyone who crossed his path. His kvelling took center stage once when I had a supporting role in a reading of a play by Israel Horovitz. After the performance my dad marched up to the playwright and said, "Isn't my daughter wonderful, beautiful, talented? Why don't you write her a bigger part?" On another day, Israel asked me the origin of the name Queller.

"Is it Spanish?"

"No," I replied. "We're Jews from Poland."

"That doesn't make sense."

"Well," I said, "my dad's cousins spell their name K-W-E-L-L-E-R. . . ."

"Of course, how fitting," Israel replied. *"Kveller."*

My dad answered the phone and right away he heard in my voice that something was wrong.

"What is it, darling?"

"There's something I have to tell you. . . ."

"I'm listening."

"Well, you know that cancer can run in families and there's this relatively new genetic test available for the so-called breast cancer gene—though the mutation also increases odds of ovarian cancer. . . . Anyway, testing positive doesn't mean you'll *definitely* get breast cancer, but it gives you up to an eighty-seven percent chance. So I took the test. And I have it."

"The bad gene?" my dad asked with controlled alarm.

"Yes." Then I quickly added, "But the good news is that Kay got her boss to let me write an article about it for the *Times!*"

Normally my dad would be elated about the article; on this day, it did not even register.

"What have the doctors advised?"

"Well, that's the thing. There are only two choices and neither is good. Undergoing close surveillance with the hope that we'll catch cancer early . . ."

"Or?"

"Mastectomy."

My father, normally never at a loss for words, was silent. Finally he asked, "What do your doctors say?"

"That I should make the decision based on my own values."

In a very quiet and serious tone my father asked me what course I wanted to take.

"I don't know."

Another heavy pause.

"I'll leave this to your judgment, sweetheart. Whatever you decide, I will support you."

IN THE SHOWER, in the writers' room, in the car, in yoga class, in bed in the dark at three a.m.—I obsessed over the potential repercussions of removing my breasts. It did not take long to conclude that my personal life would be in the most peril. If I had a mastectomy and reconstruction, would men no longer find me desirable? Would I feel deformed? Would I ever want to be touched again? Would I no longer feel like a whole woman? I'd griped about our breast-obsessed culture, but privately I'd enjoyed the admiration men expressed for my own breasts. In retrospect I found my whining hypocritical. How would I feel now, if they were gone and replaced by plastic implants and tattoos?

One sleepless night I paced around my apartment calculating time. I was thirty-five and already up against the biological clock. If I elected surgery at thirty-six, I figured it would take me about a year to recover—physically and emotionally. That meant I'd be thirty-seven when it was over. By the time I found a new boyfriend and established a relationship solid enough to get pregnant, I'd be—what, thirty-eight? Thirty-nine?

And once pregnant, postmastectomy, I would never be able to breast-feed. My mother didn't breast-feed, which was precisely why I'd always wanted to. To me, breast-feeding was the ultimate maternal act—the ability to nourish your child. I'd always looked forward to enjoying that symbiosis with my baby. Not being able to breast-feed would be a great loss.

And then there was the question of my romantic convictions. I'd witnessed many friends marry men they weren't all that crazy about because they felt it was time, only to get divorced a few years later. I'd vowed never to walk down the aisle unless I could do so with a full heart. I knew it was rare, but I held out hope that I'd find love, passion, and intellectual compatibility. In my twenties I'd always been called picky; now in my thirties, I was told I was *too* picky. When I was about twenty-five, I went on a few dates with a smart, funny character actor. My dear friend Gordon and his boyfriend met us one night for drinks. Gordon and I had been Will and Grace long before prime-time TV capitalized on that dynamic, and my boyfriends have always had to pass muster with him. The next day Gordon called for a debriefing: "He was a nice guy, but you looked so lovely and elegant and he was so nebbishy—it just seemed wrong," he said. "Besides, you can't marry an actor!" In my twenties, Gordon thought no one was good enough for me; my pickiness meant I was properly discerning. At thirty-five, Gordon was so desperate to pair me off, he didn't care *who* the guy was. Gordon had taken to making comments like "He's got shoes? Marry him." Pickiness at thirty-five is called commitment phobia—or, at best, impractical. Now try adding mastectomy to the mix. Since taking the BRCA test, I had nagging doubts for the first time that my partner would appear—never mind on schedule. If I went through with a mastectomy, could I no longer afford the luxury of being so particular?

This train of thought sent me into a tailspin. Why had I sought out this genetic information? Yes, my mother had been blindsided by cancer, but at least she'd been able to live her life according to her own values and inclinations before it struck. Was a mutant gene going to not only rob me of my breasts but defeat my ideals about love?

Or maybe this circumstance was the universe teaching me that my notions about finding a soul mate had *always* been impractical, that in order to have a family, more compromise was involved than I'd been willing to accept. I yearned to have children. *Bear* my own children. I'd been crazy about kids since I was little more than a kid myself. While other girls fantasized about their wedding day, I fantasized about being pregnant. Bearing children was not something I was willing to forgo if I had any say in the matter. As unthinkable as mastectomy was, I'd come around to considering it. I would never, ever consider having a prophylactic oophorectomy before I had children. That sacrifice was too great. Luckily, forty was generally deemed a prudent age for BRCA-positive women to have their ovaries removed, which gave me five years. If I'd tested positive for the mutation in my twenties, doctors would have recommended I have children early in life and remove my ovaries sooner. . . . I'd long missed that boat. I stopped pacing and stared out the living room window into the black Los Angeles night. If I'd been in a serious relationship now, I thought, I would have tried to have a baby right away and left cancer prevention for afterward.

There was a man—a handsome, smart, kind, talented man— who already loved me and was lurking in the wings: Jason.

Though he and I had spent little more than a weekend together before my mother died, Jason had valiantly claimed the role of my long-distance boyfriend throughout her illness. A couple of

months after her death, he flew to New York from Los Angeles
to spend his Christmas vacation working with me and Danielle in
our mother's Southampton store. Jason is a guy's guy, most at
home watching sports, drinking beer, playing poker with his bud-
dies, and yet he embraced the high-end china shop like a trouper.
He learned to distinguish the patterns of William Yeoward wine-
glasses and charmed all the ladies with his expertise: "The Fern
pattern is popular, but I prefer the Cordelia. . . ." He discovered
a latent talent for bubble-wrapping. Every day at lunchtime, he
walked down the snowy block to the deli and brought us all back
sandwiches. Jason soared at rescuing the damsel in distress, and
that's the role I'd been cast in since we'd met. We had a lovely
time that Christmas and I was moved by his warmth and generosity, yet it was emerging that the most we had in common was the
pleasure he derived in taking care of me and my great need to be
taken care of in the wake of my mom's death. I feared we were
not well matched under normal circumstances. He was five years
younger than I was and our tastes could not have been more different. He loved pop culture—reality shows, big commercial movies.
He devoured each Harry Potter book the day it hit the bookstores.
I liked foreign films and was slogging through Thomas Mann's *The
Magic Mountain* (not that I ever finished it . . .). We joked that I
was a snob, and I realized for the first time that maybe I was, but
nevertheless our sensibilities were off.

By the end of the trip, I suggested we shift our relationship and
become dear friends. Jason rejected the idea. He was convinced I
had a preconceived notion that my ideal man was an "artsy black-
turtleneck guy writing poetry in a West Village café"—but if I
could just let that go, I'd realize I was happy with him. I laughed
at Jason's caricature of "my type" and conceded it was pretty accurate. He returned to Los Angeles and to his job, and I worked

in the store for two more months. During that time, Jason and I continued to talk on the phone. He was romantic and stalwart in his feelings, and often said he wanted to marry me, though the notion was absurd—not least because we'd spent so little time together.

By early March, Danielle and I had sold off the inventory and closed up shop for good. I moved into Harriette's old apartment in Manhattan. One Friday morning, days after I'd arrived, I got a shocking call from my agent, Jeff, telling me that Adrian had committed suicide. He'd shot himself in the head. I rarely spoke of my relationship with Adrian because I felt shame about it. I knew that Adrian was an intensely dark man—I'd heard him speak of suicide—but I never believed he would actually kill himself. Just over a year ago, I'd shared a bed every night with either my mother or Adrian. Now they were both dead. I'd just managed to quiet the grief that had raged within me since my mother's death. This news brought it charging back to the surface.

Jason got on a plane that night and flew to New York to spend the weekend with me. In my heightened emotional state, I told him I would marry him. I was manic and created a plan on the spot—how did he feel about a small wedding in the Berkshires? I'd spent summers there as a teenager, it was my favorite place. . . . We could get married in July—that would give us four months to prepare and we'd invite immediate family and just a handful of friends. . . . I was on the verge of giving an inn my credit card to reserve the date when Jason suggested I wait a week or so. He was wise enough to say, "You're traumatized, Jess. I won't hold you to any of this."

About six weeks later, I moved back to Los Angeles. I got the new job on *Gilmore Girls,* a new apartment, and a new start. I decided to give my relationship with Jason a serious try. Within two months, though, it crumbled. He was a strapping, corn-fed army brat; the sports bar was his domain. I'd spent my twenties in a musical theater bar called Rose's Turn listening to gay men belt out songs from *Falsettoland*. Jason found it odd and endearing and exotic that Wallace Shawn was one of my heroes as a writer ("The guy from *The Princess Bride?*"). Jason was insanely smart—his SAT scores were leagues above mine, and he solved complex math problems in his head as a party trick. He was gorgeous and kind, and just about any girl in America would have loved to be with him. I recognized how great he was and tried to convince myself it was the right fit, while he tried to turn himself into what he thought I wanted. The relationship was off balance. I ultimately bowed out, once again.

Jason took it all in stride. We remained close. I helped him find a new apartment and furnish it. He drove me and Danielle to the animal hospital when her old yellow Lab, Coco, collapsed on the street, and he came with us to the pet cemetery to bury him.

When I tested positive for the BRCA mutation, I was once more thrust into the well-worn role of damsel in distress. True to form, Jason was there, if I chose to be rescued. He didn't grasp the preventive mastectomy concept at first, but he expressed his love and desire to stick by me—if I wanted him to—regardless of what measure I chose. I was bowled over by the goodness of this man. But was it fair to let him take care of me again? Real life had been stomping all over the place, demanding my attention. My mother had died; my biological clock was ticking; I had a mutant gene that statistically ensured I would get cancer unless I had my breasts removed. I wanted a family, and a great guy wanted to start one with me. Was I crazy to turn him down?

I was in such a panic generally that I lost all faith in my instincts. I turned to friends for advice. One faction was in the Jason camp, Gordon among them: "He's cute, smart, ambitious, he loves you—what's the problem?" Others insisted I trust myself; they said I'd soul-searched, concluded the relationship with Jason wasn't right, and must now look forward. "But . . . ," I replied, "do you understand I might have to have my breasts cut off and if I want two children—which I do—I need to have started yesterday because my ovaries need to come out, too? Suddenly the matter of my love life is urgent. What if Jason *is* the one and I'm too crazy to see it? What if I'm looking for something—for someone—who doesn't exist?" Out of pity or kindness, or to shut me up, my forward-thinking friends launched a mission to introduce me to new men.

Rebecca's office at *Gilmore Girls* was as wild and artistic as her home. Zebra-skin rugs covered the floor. A luxurious brown fake-fur blanket draped over the couch. Sheer lavender fabric was tacked above the windows, filtering the sun so the room glowed with soft, filmy light. More than a dozen framed photos and draw-ings of different shapes and sizes covered the walls. Each day I paced those zebra rugs, reciting all of my BRCA fears to Rebecca, while she brainstormed dates for me.

"You know, the guy who's most right for you is my ex-husband. . . ."

"Are you insane?"

"I know, I know. What about Mike O'Connor?"

"Sarah said he's a player. I can't go out with a player."

"We don't really know he's a player."

"Isn't he the one who tricks girls into running errands with him as a trial run before he'll take them on dates?"

"Oh yeah, forget him."

"I need someone grown-up," I said.

"I know."

"Someone ready to settle down."

"I know."

"Some brave soul who's not going to be scared of my cancer gene."

"Okay, when striking up a conversation, try not to make that your lead."

"Fine."

"And your 'I'm so old' monologue?"

"I like that monologue. . . ."

"Nix it."

Rebecca stared out of the window through the lavender gauze, flipping through a mental Rolodex.

"Wait a minute—what about Jack?" Rebecca suddenly said.

Jack was the brother and partner of Rebecca's business manager. He was in his midforties, handsome, successful, solid.

"But he's a business guy," I said to Rebecca. "Don't you think he'll be too straitlaced?"

"No, he's got a spectacular client list and jets around the world. You said you wanted a grown-up. You must go out with him."

The next day, Saturday, I had plans to spend the day with Calista and her son. It was the first time we'd had a chance to talk in person since I'd tested positive. For some reason, we wound up sitting on her bathroom floor, talking about cancer, how surreal it was that I was facing this threat, and crying. I can't tell you how we ended up there. One of us must have been washing our face or putting on makeup, while the other tagged along, when serious conversation took over. Calista told me that she'd explained my situation to her friend, an older female doctor, who felt strongly that I should have the mastectomy. Calista wept and begged me to do it. "You cannot get sick," she pleaded. The intensity of her reaction frightened me—if she was so scared on my behalf, it followed that I should be scared, too.

We made our way off the floor and downstairs to the playroom, then segued into a conversation about children. Having a son had fundamentally changed Calista's life—she was a born mother. She knew how much I wanted kids and how my clock had just sped up exponentially. She said I must absolutely have a baby right away, which led to the subject of men, which led to the revelation that Jack was also Calista's business manager.

"I love it—he's great!" she said. "Let's have a dinner party and invite him over now—tonight."

"Do you think he'd come?"

"Of course—he lives down the street. Let's wait to see if he has plans before we round up some others."

She left a casual, yet informative, message on his voice mail— "Hey, Jack, it's Calist. I'm having a few people over for dinner tonight and I want you to meet my friend *Jessica*. . . ." We started making up our guest list, planning the meal, and as the hours rolled on she called again: "Just checking in. Did you get my message? Can you come by?" We rallied friends, bought food and wine just in case, cracked open a bottle ourselves, and when there was still no word she called yet again—and was intimidating: "Okay, Jack? We just need to know whether or not you're coming!"

Finally, Jack called. He said he did have plans but would try to stop by afterward. We had a wonderful dinner, drank wine, laughed, and told our friends about our scheme. We all avidly awaited my suitor's arrival, but he never showed.

Calista's persistent messages did not go unheeded, however. Jack got my number on Monday and asked me out to dinner.

I was sprawled on the faux bear fur of Rebecca's sofa and wracked with anxiety.

"I wish I hadn't done this—I'm in no condition to go on a date. Obviously, I can't talk about the BRCA gene, but how can I *not* talk about the BRCA gene? How am I going to act normal and blasé and discuss what's going on in my life when I can't talk about what's going on in my life?"

"You used to be an actress. . . ."

"A *failed* actress."

Rebecca rolled her eyes. "You are not a failed actress."

"Jack's a *businessman*. And your brother said he's a religious Jew. Can you picture me cooking Shabbat dinner every Friday night? Keeping kosher? None of you would have fixed me up with him if I wasn't in such a rush to get married and have babies."

"But you are."

While I was getting ready for my date with Jack, my friend Liza called. We'd been roommates in London our junior year abroad and had remained close, though our lives had taken divergent paths. She'd given up a flourishing career in journalism to be a full-time mother of two in Connecticut; she lived a suburban life as remote from my urban single existence as the moon. Liza and I had been playing phone tag for ages, so I picked up to talk briefly as I did my makeup. Liza's tone was serious and full of concern. As with Calista, we hadn't yet had a chance to discuss my bad gene. Liza told me she'd gotten two calls in the same week—one from me saying I had the BRCA mutation and one from her high school friend Julie saying she had breast cancer. I put down my mascara. Once again, I found myself sitting on a bathroom floor. Liza said Julie (who was our age) had discovered a lump while breast-feeding. She was about to start chemo. "I'm so sorry about your gene, Jess. But I'm so happy you don't have cancer."

I had agreed to meet Jack at a fancy Italian restaurant in Beverly Hills. As I drove, I thought about Liza's friend. I remembered Liza telling stories about her—Julie had been one of the prettiest, most popular girls in their high school class. Had she maybe been a cheerleader . . . ? I tried to fathom that we were no longer girls dealing with problems like who was going to take us to the prom, but women grappling with illness. As I neared Beverly Hills, I started to focus on my date. I was nervous. How was I going to do this? How was I going to be charming and normal with my head full of death and doom? I started singing in the car to get my energy up. I belted out Patsy Kline's "Crazy"—maybe not the best choice. I told myself there was no reason I couldn't summon bright energy at will.

Jack was as described—handsome, wearing a suit, very much a man (not a boy). I was overcompensating from the start—being a bit too talkative—yet I managed to maintain some poise. After the second glass of wine my facade started cracking. Kay had often remarked with amusement that whenever I'm feeling nervous or ungrounded my theater training kicks in. My voice projects, my passions become large. I either *hate* someone or *love* them. In truth, that's always my temperament, but on such occasions it becomes amplified. Jack and I discovered we knew several people in common and I was less than politic.

"You wrote on that show?" Jack asked. "Did you know Brian Katz?"

"Yes! Spineless, lily-livered lapdog! He followed our witch of a boss around shamelessly—what a sycophant! He elevated the role of yes-man to an art form."

"He's my best friend."

Needless to say, Jack never called me again.

FOURTEEN

was embarrassed by my date with Jack. I'd always strived for the grace of Natalie Wood and here I was, transformed by stress and anxiety into a monstrous, histrionic Joan Crawford. Jack had opted out, I was later told, because I was "too much drama." I felt so much pressure in my personal life—yet how would I ever get close to someone in this frantic state?

Jason was never completely out of the picture. We talked regularly and had dinner or went to the movies every week or so. Getting back together remained a possibility, and I thought about it constantly. I couldn't decide whether I'd left him for the right reasons or if I had an unrealistic notion of what meeting the right person would feel like.

In the meantime, I managed to finish a draft of the Op-Ed piece. Kay showed it to her boss, who was enthusiastic. He gave some notes, and I completed a second draft within the week. It was accepted for publication, and Kay was assigned as editor. It seemed unreal. Kay would do an edit and e-mail it to me; I'd make changes and send it back. This exchange went on for two weeks. We were used to e-mailing long rants to each other several times a day, so working on the article felt like an extension of our normal dialogue. It was just me and Kay making stuff up. I couldn't believe that it would actually run in the *Times*. After a while, Kay started getting crabby. She said that a writer would usually only get to comment on an edit once—I'd been through half a dozen drafts. She sent me the final edit and told me I could make no further comments. I read it and freaked out. I had not yet decided what to do in the wake of learning my BRCA status, so my article merely posed the big questions. In this latest version, Kay had changed a sentence about considering mastectomy as an option to an emphatic statement that I *would,* in fact, have a mastectomy. I called Kay, outraged and panicked.

"What is it?" she answered. "I told you we're not making any more changes."

"You changed the content of a sentence—I never wrote that I intended to have a mastectomy!"

"If you don't take a stand, there's no thesis to the article."

"I haven't made up my mind yet and I'm certainly not ready to announce to the whole world that I'm going to cut my breasts off!"

"Well, then, maybe we should pull the article until you are."

Kay had no hesitation in using any tactic to prod me into surgery. However, she did restore the line as I'd written it and submitted the piece. It was set to run a few days later, barring the death of a world leader, a natural disaster, a terrorist attack, or some other surprise event of national importance that would bump my piece.

Around this time I had a phone session with Mark Epstein,

my sometime therapist. We hadn't spoken in a while, though I'd e-mailed him about my BRCA status. I told him about the article and how, now that I'd written it, I was experiencing some buyer's remorse. What had I been thinking—announcing to the world that I was considering a mastectomy? I was worried that I'd gotten caught up in all the research and fear. Maybe I'd been rash in writing the article, maybe I'd been alarmist in my evaluation of the whole topic. "When it comes down to it," I said, "I can't fathom actually going through with surgery—"

Mark interrupted. "You have to do it."

"I do?"

"Absolutely. There is no question."

Mark is a psychiatrist, an MD. He'd attended Harvard Medical School and spoke with the authority of a physician.

"You're definite about this?"

"Yes."

"Why are you so definite about this?"

"I'm about ten years older than you, Jessica. Between thirty-five and forty-five, many of my friends got breast cancer. I watched a lot of them die."

"But, Mark, single women my age are not really doing this. . . ."

"That's only because the test is relatively new."

"Married women with kids? Yes. But women in my position? No. It's not being done."

"So you'll be the vanguard."

Though I'd been circling the idea of mastectomy for months, Mark Epstein's forceful directive unhinged me. It was one thing to debate the issue philosophically. It was quite another to check myself into a hospital and do it. In spite of the statistics, I did *not* have cancer. What if I lopped off my breasts and turned out to be one of the BRCA-positive women whose mutation never caused illness? Even as I posed that question, I knew it was moot. I'd be taking a huge risk to find out whether I was one of the lucky few, and I wasn't a gambler. My mood turned from frantic to edgy. I was feeling trapped.

I checked my e-mail one morning from my office at *Gilmore Girls* and saw that the Writers Guild of America was offering a seminar the following evening called "The New Genetics: Progress, Promises, and Pitfalls." The focus of the evening would be BRCA mutations and prenatal genetic testing. I almost always deleted e-mails from the WGA without reading them, and thought it was uncanny that I'd opened this one—weird, too, that they were presenting the topic at all. I decided to attend and asked Jason to come with me. I'd been gravitating toward Jason emotionally again, wondering still whether we could work. This seminar was a good opportunity to see how it felt to have him by my side while I faced BRCA issues.

Jason and I entered the large room. There was a dais in the front for panelists and rows of folding chairs for the audience. I'd been a member of the guild for five years but had never been to one of these things. As we took our seats, I remarked to Jason how nice it was that the WGA presented medical issues that might be of concern to its members. As the first geneticist spoke, I noticed that quite a few people in the audience were taking notes. Then I overheard one guy say to another, "This would make a great B-story. . . ." Suddenly, it dawned on me: the purpose of the evening was to educate writers on these subjects so they could portray them on TV. I was no doubt the only writer there for personal reasons.

This realization left me feeling vulnerable. I glanced through the program. It had a list of facts about BRCA mutations, one of which—I knew from my research—was incorrect. I whispered to Jason, "This is a mistake."

"Don't point it out to them, don't say anything," he said, and I stiffened. "I don't want you to make a scene or embarrass anyone."

I was hurt and angry. Did he really think I would humiliate a panelist? I felt inhibited and self-conscious. Whatever I might have to add to this forum would be relevant—but I knew now that I would not speak. I pulled away from Jason, regretting that I had invited him, feeling alone.

When I shut down to Jason, he made no move to hold my hand or make things better. We sat side by side in icy tension, and I was barely able to concentrate on the speakers. What I did hear was all familiar—I'd been researching, writing, and talking about nothing else for months. I did not raise my hand during the time allotted for questions, but after the seminar was over, I approached the panel while Jason stood awkwardly off to the side. I introduced myself to the moderator, Neal Baer—a wonderful man who's both a doctor and a veteran TV writer. I also introduced myself to a genetic oncologist from the National Cancer Institute in Washington, D.C.—the premier cancer research hospital in the country. I briefed the doctor on my story and asked him the essential question: "If I were your daughter or your wife, what course of action would you recommend?" The NCI oncologist took a weighty pause, then replied: "I'd tell you to have the mastectomy."

I was in a black mood when we left the building. Jason and I fought—one of the few times we ever did. In the end we both apologized and I conceded that the BRCA topic was so incendiary for me that anyone who had come along to the seminar would have been in a danger zone. Though we made up—and I believed I'd been too hard on him—my feeling of isolation remained. I did not sleep that night. I didn't know which way things would go with Jason, but I felt that making any bold moves in my love life right now would be a mistake. For the time being, I decided not to decide.

MY FRIEND STEPHEN called to let me know that his friend's wife was BRCA-positive and had recently undergone a prophylactic double mastectomy and reconstruction. Suzy Hurley lived in Los Angeles and told Stephen she'd be happy to talk to me. I hadn't yet met anyone who had actually gone through this, so I eagerly set a date to meet her at the Coffee Bean & Tea Leaf on Larchmont Boulevard.

I arrived first and grabbed a table. A beautiful blond in a tank top walked through the door, looked at me, and said, "Jessica?" Suzy was a few years older than I and looked terrific. She sat down and we became so instantly immersed in conversation that we never got around to ordering coffee.

Suzy told me her story. She had grown up in a small town in Missouri with four sisters and two brothers. Suzy and her twin sister, Sally, were the youngest; their sister Kerry was a year and a half older. In 1999, at age thirty-four, Kerry discovered a lump in her breast. By the time she noticed it, the tumor was so big it was visible. Kerry went in for a mammogram and an ultrasound (MRI was not yet available), and her doctors told her it didn't look like cancer. However, a breast surgeon performed a needle biopsy just to be sure, and discovered that, in fact, the tumor was malignant.

Kerry had to decide quickly whether to have a lumpectomy or

a single mastectomy. The oncologist said she had strong odds of a recurrence, so she opted for mastectomy. After her operation, the surgeon informed her that the cancer had not spread to her lymph nodes; however, it was an aggressive form of cancer and she would have to begin chemotherapy immediately.

Kerry asked why the cancer had not been recognized on her mammogram. She was told that mammograms don't give very accurate readings for premenopausal women with dense breast tissue.

Shortly after her surgery, while at the University of Kansas Medical Center, Kerry learned about the BRCA test. She wanted to take it, but the doctors discouraged her, saying there was not enough cancer in her family to warrant it. Kerry's mother had never had cancer, nor had her grandmothers or sisters. Kerry's aunt—her father's sister—was the only relative with a history of the disease. Kerry insisted on taking the test anyway. She needed to know if there was an explanation for why she'd gotten cancer at such a young age.

Her instincts were right—she tested positive for BRCA-1. Soon after, a spot was found on her ovaries. The doctors had no way of knowing whether it was cancer until they operated. Kerry was frantic and chose to have a full hysterectomy and a mastectomy on her second breast at the same time. For her first breast reconstruction, Kerry had opted for a TRAM flap, using tummy fat rather than an implant. The procedure had been excruciating, so for the second side, she chose a saline implant. Because she'd used two different methods of reconstruction, her breasts turned out to be different shapes and sizes.

That Christmas, Kerry's large family gathered around her. She had lost all her hair to chemo and was very sick. Her small children didn't want her to pick them up from school because of how she looked. Her daughter had developed a rash on her face and neck from nerves.

The day after Christmas, Kerry's parents and siblings decided to go en masse to the genetics department at the University of Kansas to be tested for the BRCA mutation. Suzy was the only other sibling to test positive. Their father tested positive as well.

Meanwhile, Suzy had already discovered a lump in her breast and had told no one.

Suzy went to see a female breast surgeon in Los Angeles who felt her lump and told her bluntly: "Because of your BRCA status, you need to have a double mastectomy. Here are the names of some plastic surgeons." The doctor handed her a stack of business cards and left the examining room to attend to another patient. Suzy burst into tears. She had known about her BRCA status for maybe a week. The idea of mastectomy was horrific, unthinkable —how could this surgeon just matter-of-factly sentence her to this fate? When the doctor returned to find Suzy weeping, she apologized for her abruptness. The doctor explained that her own sister had undergone breast surgery that very day. Their family had a strong history of breast cancer, yet her sister had refused to take the BRCA test and now had cancer with a poor prognosis.

Suzy left the office traumatized. She hadn't had a biopsy and still didn't know whether her lump was cancer.

Soon after, she made an appointment with a different breast surgeon. He examined her and found a *second* lump. Mammogram and ultrasound results were inconclusive. The surgeon said that he could do two lumpectomies, but if the tumors proved to be benign, she would continue to have lumps and scares regularly because, like her sister, Suzy had dense breast tissue.

"You have the only preventable cancer, Suzy," he said. "You don't know what I see every day. I am powerless to help these people."

This is what persuaded Suzy to schedule a prophylactic double mastectomy. She scheduled a hysterectomy at the same time. She was thirty-seven and the mother of two little girls when she had the operations.

I listened, riveted, and then bombarded her with questions: Was surgery painful? Was it psychologically traumatic? How long did it take to recover? Did it impair her range of movement? What kind of reconstruction did she choose? How did she like the results? And what about her sex life? How did her husband react?

Suzy said it had been very hard for her husband to grasp the necessity for the surgery. It wasn't something he'd ever heard of before. A mastectomy without cancer seemed bafflingly radical. Neither of them knew of anyone who had been through it (though Suzy contacted women through FORCE before her operation). There was no frame of reference. Her husband was supportive in that he, of course, did not want her to get cancer. But some days he just couldn't cope with what was happening. Suzy's family flew to Los Angeles to help take care of the children. Her husband remained shell-shocked throughout her recovery.

Suzy said she was just as emotional about losing her uterus as she was about losing her breasts. She mourned the loss of that part of her body where her little girls had lived before they were born. It took her several months to recover fully and be able to care for her kids the way she used to, but she insisted that the primary emotion she felt after the surgery was relief—intense relief that she was no longer a ticking time bomb.

Suzy had opted for silicone implants. She said she was afraid she was going to look like just another fake blond with fake boobs in Hollywood, but the surgeon did a good job and she was quite happy with them. She felt natural and sexy in her new body. Her range of movement was entirely restored—she was a gymnast and was once again doing back handsprings.

"I wore a tank top on purpose so you could see how normal I'm still able to dress. Do you want to see my breasts?"

"I would love to."

We walked down the block to a clothing store called Picket Fences and ducked into a dressing room. Suzy took off her shirt.

Her breasts looked astonishingly real. Of course, she had mastectomy scars, but they were faint. After staring at them for a while, I noticed a barely discernible, slight rippling at the edge of one of her breasts. A woman who elects cosmetic breast surgery has real breast tissue to cushion the implants, whereas a woman who has a mastectomy has only a thin layer of muscle and skin to hide the plastic casing. Overall, I felt heartened. Suzy didn't look scary or deformed—her breasts were beautiful.

"Touch them—don't they feel real?"

We giggled as I touched my new friend's new fake boobs.

"Wow, they do feel real!" I said.

I was so moved that a woman I'd known for only an hour had openly shared something this intimate with me. My time with Suzy felt like an initiation. It made the operation tangible and real. And for the first time I thought: Maybe I can do this.

FIFTEEN

Most television writers' rooms consist of a conference table and a dozen industrial desk chairs. The *Gilmore Girls* room was the exception. Overstuffed sofas arranged on a plush rug reminded me of the lavish Hollywood Hills living rooms I used to frequent when I first moved to Los Angeles. New in town, I said yes to all invitations and regularly drove up treacherous roads to some grand house or other for a cocktail party hosted by a friend of a friend's cousin who was invariably a high-powered producer or studio executive. The only prop that belied the function of the *Gilmore Girls* writers' room was the dry-erase board that covered the length of a wall. Amy Sherman-Palladino was the creator of the show, and generic offices were not her style. She insisted that every nook of her domain match her outsized personality. Even the common bathroom was transformed into a frilly powder room—lotions in pretty bottles, candles, and exotic soaps lined the shelves. Amy herself was short with porcelain skin and jet black hair cropped at the shoulders. She dressed in outfits that harked back to the East Village of the 1980s—Betsy Johnson crinoline skirts with leggings, tight layered T-shirts, and, on occasion, a top hat. Amy's office was a hybrid of French boudoir and kitsch. A chartreuse-colored divan swooned under the windows. Fringed lamps emitted amber light. Several stools covered with hot pink muppet fur were scattered around the room. The ceiling was painted in squares of discordant colors—purple, green, pink, blue. In the corner, a life-size mannequin posed in a Girl Scout uniform.

On a Friday afternoon when the whole writing staff was assembled, a woman from the *New York Times* called the office asking for me. One of the *Gilmore* producers continued outlining scenes on the board, while I picked up the extension on the far side of the room. The woman from the *Times* told me she was faxing over a contract for me to initial and sign. My article would be running the next day, in Saturday's paper. My stomach dropped. My gratification over having completed the article was eclipsed by the sick feeling that I was about to be publicly exposed and there was no turning back. It was worse than the classic nightmare scenario of finding yourself standing onstage in your underwear. I would be onstage, naked from the waist up for all the world to see. My mother's admonishment rang in my ears: "Never pose topless!" Strangers would stare at my breasts in morbid fascination.

When I hung up with the *Times,* Amy and her husband, Dan, my bosses, looked up with interest. "What was that about?"

For months, everyone who'd come through our offices had been subjected, ad nauseum, to my rants about the BRCA mutation. It was hard to believe this was the first Amy and Dan had heard of it, yet when I told them about my predicament and the article it spawned, they screwed up their faces in surprise. Amy looked at me in faux disbelief and asked, "Can't you just dip your boobs in green tea?"

I'd experienced a strange phenomenon on every one of my writing jobs—as a general rule, the sweeter the television show, the meaner the bosses. Contrary to the cozy tone of *Gilmore Girls,* Amy and Dan were not what you would call warm. Amy openly identified with Darth Vader—something about how all of his underlings were incompetent, so of course the poor misunderstood guy had to kill them off, just as she'd been driven to fire a slew of employees. Ayn Rand was Amy's moral authority: People with talent rose to the top, those without it perished, and thus the universe was ruthless and just. All in all, the green tea comment was rather tame.

Rebecca was as excited about the Op-Ed piece as if she'd written it herself. The moment we left the room, she burst out: "Jess, do you realize what a big deal this is? It's not 'Rory got drunk for the first time over spring break and, my heavens, will Lorelai's remedy of greasy fries work for the next generation of Gilmore hangovers?' It's real, it's about illness and life and what matters and it's your own and Oh My God it's the *New York Times!*"

That night I went out for sushi with my sister. Danielle looked polished and perfect in leggings and a pearl gray shawl, while I was haggard and wild-eyed. Danielle even made yoga leggings look glamorous—she had that ineffable quality passed down from our mother. Though I'd approached fashion with a new vigor since my mom's death, putting myself together remained work for me, a chore. I could buy the designer dress, but I could never carry it off like Danielle. I would always have a label sticking out, a fraying hem, a rip in the seam. I had certainly not inherited the glamour gene that could be traced in a direct line from Harriette to Stephanie to Danielle.

It's worth mentioning that my attitude toward material beauty had recently changed in more ways than one. In my early twenties, when I was hurt over what I perceived as my mother's lack of maternal interest in me, I was judgmental about her passion for *things*. I saw her interests and pursuits as shallow. As she blossomed as a mom through her illness, my anger melted away and, with it, my disdain for the material things she loved. More than that, I now viewed my mother's quest for beauty—in her appearance, her life, her work—not as superficial, but as an expression of her immense vitality. In the past I had dismissed her as shallow. I now perceived her in grand terms—a force of nature, deeply driven and utterly human. Her passion to create beauty was anything but trivial—it was the language in which she expressed her love of life.

Danielle and I sat at a small table in the Japanese restaurant. I was feeling neurotic and insecure. "What on earth spurred me to write about something this intimate?" I asked, downing hot sake. I rattled on about all the possible repercussions of the article. I pictured acquaintances reading the morning paper and choking on their cereal. I had dark thoughts about the pleasure my travails would give those who did not wish me well. I imagined Adrian's wife thinking: *Serves her right—she behaved badly and now she has to cut her breasts off as penance.*

I speculated that maybe, on a subconscious level, I'd expressed my dilemma in a public way in order to push myself into the mastectomy. "Mom endured such horror and torment—God knows I don't want cancer. But removing my breasts is so intense, so extreme—maybe I had to put the concept of mastectomy-as-responsible-choice out in the world to shame myself into doing it. But can I really go through with it . . . ?" I blathered on, repeating everything I'd already said a thousand times, and Dani listened patiently. Eventually, I talked myself full-circle, back to the piece in the *Times*. "Will you e-mail some of Mom's friends tonight? Alert them about tomorrow's article? I write about Mom at length and I think it would be meaningful for them to read."

Dani's composure finally broke.

"What's wrong?" I asked.

Her voice shook with barely contained anger. "I didn't want to bring this up, because writing about it has been your process, but I am *not* comfortable with the whole thing. Your taking the test has canceled out my choice to remain sheltered from all of this. And your writing about it has taken away my privacy. I do *not* want to bring attention to the article. I just want it to pass as quickly as possible. I haven't mentioned this sooner because, thankfully, most of my friends don't read the Op-Ed page of the *New York Times*."

I sat in stunned silence.

"I'm so sorry. I didn't realize—"

"It's fine. It's what you needed to do."

I stayed over at Danielle's apartment that night, but didn't sleep at all. Lying awake, I considered Danielle's situation and my own. I had not shown her the article even though she was featured in it. The central questions the article posed—Was knowledge power or ignorance bliss? Biotechnology now offered us the ability to know what diseases were in store for us, but was this helpful information?—were questions just as relevant to her life as they were to mine. In the piece I discussed the pros and cons of choosing knowledge over ignorance. With two imperfect choices, I'd elected to be forewarned of disease, while my sister had elected not to take the test, not to be burdened with knowledge.

Danielle was right. I had opened up her life for speculation by disclosing her choice.

I left early the next morning. I'd imagined we would buy the paper and read it together over breakfast, but now I felt awkward and guilty. I hadn't thought through how I was dragging her into this, and I certainly hadn't been sensitive to her feelings.

Bleary but wired, I drove to the newsstand on La Brea and bought a copy of the paper. March 5, 2005. I opened it in the parking lot. The illustration on the Op-Ed page made me gasp: a girl's head superimposed over the form of an older woman with a serpent rising within her. Daughter and mother and snake as illness. It was powerful, dark, and beautiful. My article ran beneath it. Kay had told me there would be artwork, but I could never have imagined something this arresting.

The rest of the day was a blur. It felt like everyone I'd ever known was calling or e-mailing. Some people were shocked, others were moved, and still others expressed their profound sympathy. All said they could not fathom my dilemma. My dad was bursting with pride (kvelling). He called every ten minutes to inform me who had just read the article. "Marvin and Ethel called; Uncle Lee and Auntie Fran; your cousins Michael and Stacey; and you remember my friend Shelly Fireman? He owns Shelley's in New York and a dozen other A-class restaurants? He read the article in the *International Herald Tribune* from his villa in Tuscany!" Then Danielle called. Her tone had changed entirely—she was quiet and warm. She said she'd been deeply affected by the piece and had composed an e-mail to a dozen of her closest friends—in addition to friends of our mom's—proudly telling them to read her sister's article. That was the greatest gift of the day.

That weekend, Danielle reported that the fancy New York City Jewish ladies were talking of nothing but the Op-Ed. Many of them knew our mother, many more were breast cancer survivors, and most had never heard of the BRCA test. Should they take it? What about their daughters? Everyone I spoke to told me the article had sparked passionate debate among family and friends. The resounding question: If they found themselves in my shoes, what would they do? Would they choose to know their genetic status or not to know? It seemed that people strongly gravitated to one side or the other, just like me and Danielle.

At work on Monday, Amy entered the writers' room in a blur of excitement. "Howard Stern was talking about Jessica on the radio! Robyn brought up this article about a girl having to decide whether to cut her boobs off, and Howard and Artie chimed in, and I was like—holy shit—they're talking about Jessica! That is so fucking cool!"

Dan Palladino complimented me on the article two times. From Amy and Dan, this was an onslaught of approbation.

I continued to get messages from people I knew, people I barely knew, and people I didn't know at all. I got e-mails from friends of friends who had similar histories of cancer in their families, asking questions and soliciting advice. People contacted me to share their personal breast cancer stories. Someone who identified himself as a doctor from Australia repeatedly called the *Gilmore Girls* office saying he had to stop me before I did anything rash because he'd invented a concoction of mushrooms that prevented cancer. Friends told me they'd forwarded my article to other friends who were at high risk to inspire them to take the test. My agent Jeff called multiple times. *Good Morning America* had contacted William Morris because they had a piece on breast cancer and genetics set to go but didn't have a face to personalize it—could they interview me? They would send a film crew over to put me on tape the next morning at around five a.m. A documentary filmmaker wanted to follow me and Danielle and chronicle our medical journeys. A producer from *Nightline* called—would I agree to do a segment? And the literary division of William Morris in New York called—would I want to write a book?

To all of this Kay said: "Ah, the reach of the *New York Times*. . . ."

All of this attention made one thing abundantly clear: The predicament I faced truly was new and shocking. It was uncharted territory and it had struck a collective nerve.

I hadn't slept in days and couldn't see straight. I told Jeff I could not appear on *Good Morning America* the next day. I'd trip over my words, say crazy things, and be of no use to the cause of women's cancer prevention. A documentary? Not in a million years. I hated cameras; being followed by one would be exquisite torture. I asked Jeff what he thought I should do. He suggested I spend some time thinking about whether I'd want to write further about this topic, to consider the idea of writing a book. And he thought it would be worthwhile to do one substantive interview. I returned the call from the producer at *Nightline,* a young woman my age named Courtney. We hit it off right away; she was smart and empathetic and down to earth. Courtney had read the article and wanted to find out if I'd be interested in doing an interview before she pitched it to her boss. As it happened, my friend Liza's mother-in-law is the journalist Cokie Roberts, herself a breast cancer survivor. When I had frantically been researching BRCA, Liza had put me in touch with Cokie. We spoke on the phone, and I later called her oncologist at the National Cancer Institute for advice. I knew Cokie Roberts had worked on *Nightline* and assumed she had alerted Courtney of the article. "No," Courtney said, "but I do know her, and she occasionally still does interviews for us. Maybe she would do this one." I called Liza, who called Cokie, who immediately agreed to do it. The next thing I knew, I'd signed up for an appearance on *Nightline.*

After the hoopla died down, I was left with myself and my breast cancer gene. The *Nightline* interview was scheduled for late

April, six weeks away. "You'd better figure out what course of action you're going to take before you go on national television," Kay said. I did not respond.

I'd been spending a lot of time lately reading the FORCE message boards, but I still considered myself a voyeur rather than a participant. I had never posted a question; I had anonymously been reading threads about the different methods of breast reconstruction. There were so many choices, it was dizzying. The two major categories were autogenous reconstruction and implant reconstruction. The first uses your own body's tissue to reconstruct the breasts, and I was astonished by how many body sites you could snag tissue from. Doctors could create "flaps" from the tummy, the tush, the back, the thigh. Let's say you zeroed in on an area—settled on donating your excess stomach fat to the cause—oh, the choices that remained! The menu was as long and nuanced as Starbucks'. Are you a venti, nonfat, decaf carmel macchiato kind of girl? Perhaps you'd like attached flaps—your stomach fat and muscle will be slid under the skin to the mastectomy site and shaped into breasts while remaining attached by a strip of muscle to its original blood supply. Or are you a tazo iced chai latte with soy milk type? Then free flaps could be for you—tummy fat with only a small portion of muscle completely removed from the donor site and transplanted to the chest. Maybe you're a classic café Americano drinker—perforator flaps are the way to go: use of abdominal skin and fat without sacrificing any muscle, carefully dissected by a skilled microsurgeon and reconnected to the chest's blood vessels. Implant reconstruction had no fewer options. There was the two-step expander-reconstruction process or the cutting-edge one-step alloderm procedure. Treatises had been written on the matter of silicone versus saline implants. I read the FORCE site regularly, but I read from a safe distance. I could not identify myself as one of them. The procedures were too graphic, too brutal. I could not yet make the leap.

A few days later, I received a letter in the mail. It had been addressed to me, care of my father's law office, and forwarded to me by his secretary.

Dear Jessica Queller,

I read your piece in the New York Times. *It was so good and something that so many women are forced to ponder.*

I'm writing because I knew your mother, Stephanie, and was so sad last year when I saw that she had died (I read an obituary in the Times) *and then because we had the same surgeon I asked Dr. Daniel Roses on my next visit was it really Stephanie who had died? I knew, but didn't want to know—cliché though that sounds. And Dr. Roses is a great surgeon and professional beyond words, but he is an uptight, precise, and at times "detached" man. Yet when I asked him about your mother—it was the first time in nearly eleven years that he paused, his face and the tone of his voice changed and he actually stood facing me. He became quite emotional as he spoke about your mother—how much she meant to him and other doctors at NYU and that "she had extraordinary daughters. They are wonderful women," he said. Any patient of Dr. Roses knows the "routine" (if one can say going for a lifetime's worth of six-month checkups for breast cancer is routine) of Dr. Roses coming into the examining room, saying a few words and conducting a very quick but thorough exam and then exiting. I know your mother would know what I am talking about. However, as I said, this was the first time that I saw him as a man and not a surgeon—a man who knew how special your mother was.*

I met your mother and father one Saturday morning in the week following both your mother's and my breast cancer surgeries. Both

your mother and I (and your father) were waiting for Dr. Roses,
who was making a special visit to his office on a weekend morning
because both your mother and I needed to be drained. I'm sure you
know what this means. (For a time after breast cancer surgery there
is a huge amount of lymphatic fluid that is constantly collecting
and thus must be drained.) I had just turned forty and my third son
was twelve months old. Your mother was fifty. Right away we liked
one another and we were the first "breast cancer friends" one another
had come into contact with in the days following our surgeries. Also,
I am not a "political breast cancer patient." I don't go on marches
and don't seek out other women who have had breast cancer. I don't
wear a pink baseball cap and a Susan Komen T-shirt. It just isn't
me. I got the feeling that your mother, too (as we stood outside
Dr. Roses's office waiting for him to arrive), was a more discreet
person and not one to devote her life to being a "survivor" (a word I
really don't like). I think that is just one of the reasons I liked her
so much and why she struck me. She was optimistic that morning,
funny, nervous, and anxious (we both were)—but still upbeat and
she talked about her job and you and your sister. Also, your
mother was just beautiful. And she was so sweet in her beauty
and so humble being that she had a very important and high-
powered job.

The following Saturday morning again—your mother and father
and I found ourselves at the hospital very early and thus we all sat
in the downstairs waiting area of NYU to again wait for Dr. Roses.
By this time the fact that your mother and I were beginning to
truly try and wrap our minds around the fact that we had cancer
was more evident. Too, in the week since we had seen one another
we had both been to see the same oncologist for the first time and
the prospect of upcoming chemotherapy had both your mother and
I much more agitated, scared, and helpless this day. Yet we found

such comfort in one another. We practically ran into one another's arms in the lobby that day. I was wearing a wig over my long brown hair. After my visit to the oncologist that week I had run out and bought two very expensive long-brown-haired wigs from the fanciest store on 57th Street. I told your mother that it was exactly what the oncologist had not advised. "Don't go out and spend a lot of money on a wig," she had said. And with that I did just the opposite. I told your mother this and she understood completely and we laughed. Both of us were vain and cared about how we looked. We went into a ladies' room together while your father sat outside reading the New York Times and like two teenagers we nervously giggled and I showed her my wig in detail. (As it turned out I ended up with an oncologist from Mount Sinai and he recommended a less potent chemotherapy and I never ended up losing my hair. It thinned out a bit and I was sick as a dog after every infusion, but I didn't have to go through that horrifying result of chemotherapy.) After we saw Dr. Roses that morning we traded phone numbers. I never saw your mother again, but for three years we stayed in constant phone contact. As busy as your mother was she ALWAYS called me and she ALWAYS returned my calls.

After your mother's first chemotherapy treatment I called her. She was so cute on the phone. She laughed and told me that she and your father had ordered Chinese food that night and told me how strange it tasted. She made some very funny analogy which I don't remember. What I do remember is how relaxed and accepting she was of what she had gone through that day for the first time.

In many of our phone calls your mother indicated how concerned she was about her "girls." That seemed to be foremost on her mind—that she didn't want you and your sister to worry nor have added stress in your lives.

I never saw your mother again after that second time at the

hospital waiting for Dr. Roses, but she was so important in my life—as a buddy. We talked about many things other than our health. We shared stories about our children, New York City, jobs, marriages—the gamut. Three years later I had a recurrence of breast cancer and though it had appeared in my left breast again I opted to have a double radical mastectomy with reconstruction that took two and a half years. I didn't want to bring your mother down with my news so we lost touch after that. Then, as I said, I saw the obituary listing last year in the Times. I was so upset that I did something that may sound "sick," but in a way it shows what an effect your mother and her spirit had on me. I didn't want to believe that it was the same Stephanie Queller and so I called her cell phone. Her voice was on the recording and thus until I saw Dr. Roses a few weeks later as I wrote to you already I went around believing that your mother had not died. It is strange in life . . . a dear relative might die and one doesn't shed a tear and yet the death of someone whom one didn't know for a long time, someone who one met incidentally, can be far more heartbreaking.

I had always wanted to write to you and your sister, but you wouldn't know who the hell I was. So when I saw your piece in yesterday's Times I felt sad, but also blessed that perhaps now I could write to you and tell you that I loved your mother and how much she meant to me. And because I was ten or eleven years younger she treated me as a friend, but also in a motherly way— especially because I had a twelve-year-old son and two babies in diapers.

Please know that I am and have always thought about you and your sister and your dear mother for a long time and always will.

With much love,
Liza Wherry

After reading this letter, I wept the whole night.

The next morning I set up appointments to interview breast surgeons.

My friend Kelly came with me to see the first doctor. Kelly and I had acted in a play together right out of college; she'd been a far more experienced actress than I and had taken me under her wing. I'd known her two little boys since they were born and was uncommonly close with them. Whenever I wanted a real meal or the comfort of home, I went to Kelly's house. She was my family in Los Angeles. Dr. Anderson was a veteran surgeon with an excellent reputation. Soft-spoken and articulate with sparkling, intelligent eyes, Dr. Anderson was straight out of central casting as the wise, venerable doctor. I felt immediately at ease. His breadth of knowledge on the BRCA mutation was vast. He spent two hours answering my questions. I wanted to know if I was being melodramatic. By this point, many doctors had recommended mastectomy, but what was the truth about vigilant screening? How effective was it really? Had I gotten carried away with my research and convinced myself that I needed to take this drastic measure, when screening was the more rational choice?

Dr. Anderson assured me that I was not being overly dramatic. Though surveillance was a reasonable choice, it would always carry with it a strong level of uncertainty. Even if mammography or MRI detects a tumor at its earliest stage, there are certain types of aggressive cancer that start spreading the moment the cells are malignant. Regardless of how careful the screening, there would never be a way of ensuring that a found cancer would not require chemo or hadn't already spread.

"Suppose I did surveillance and we spotted cancer at the earliest stage, and let's assume it was not invasive. In that best-case scenario, what would the treatment be?"

Dr. Anderson said at minimum I would have a lumpectomy and radiation. However, if the cancer returned, or if a new primary cancer developed, and I opted for double mastectomy and reconstruction down the line, it would be much trickier cosmetically because radiated skin is difficult to work with. Radiated skin is much more likely to form a hard capsule around an implant. Also, being BRCA-1-positive means that the residual breast tissue after a lumpectomy may still carry the 87 percent chance of cancer. Given those odds, once I got breast cancer, mastectomy would be recommended. I turned to Kelly. Was there a point in doing surveillance, waiting for cancer to strike, and then getting a mastectomy anyway? In that case, I would always have to live with the threat of a recurrence—that one renegade cancer cell had been left behind and would resurface somewhere else in my body. Was that worth a few more years of natural breasts?

Dr. Anderson told me that Dr. Susan Love, the famous breast cancer surgeon and author, had long been the strongest opponent of preventive mastectomy. Her argument was that no surgeon could get every single breast cell out—some tissue would always remain. And if every cell carries the elevated risk of cancer, what was the point of surgery? She contended that the risk of breast cancer was a question not of how much breast tissue you have, but of how much whatever tissue you *do* have is acted on by carcinogens and other factors that cause cancer. The counterargument was that removing vast amounts of breast tissue would dramatically decrease the odds of cancer. Once the data came out from recent BRCA studies confirming this, Dr. Love publicly announced that she stood corrected: Preventive mastectomy is undeniably effective.

I had been harping for months on the psychological downsides to mastectomy. We now spoke about the psychological benefits. If I chose surveillance, I would continue to have scares because of my naturally dense, cystic breasts. I would fear every lump was cancer. I would likely be subjected to many biopsies and probably lumpectomies in doctors' vigilance to rule out cancer. I would always be waiting for the other shoe to drop; I would be subjected to emotionally exhausting tests every three months.

"That's one of the reasons my friend Suzy decided to go forward with prophylactic mastectomy. She didn't want to agonize over every lump for the rest of her life. She didn't want to be terrorized by fear," I said.

I asked Dr. Anderson about the statistics. Everything I'd read stated that prophylactic mastectomy decreases the odds of breast cancer by 90 percent, not 100. Still, a 10 percent chance of breast cancer even after undergoing a radical mastectomy was not minuscule. Every woman in America has a 10 percent chance of getting breast cancer. Dr. Anderson spent a good deal of time emphasizing the necessity of a very meticulous, thorough mastectomy. "That's the art of it," he said. "It is crucial to choose a surgeon who is aggressive, who will remove every bit of tissue possible." In Dr. Anderson's opinion, for a woman operated on by an excellent surgeon, the odds of getting breast cancer would be closer to 3 percent than 10, though data did not yet exist to back that up.

Last, we spoke of what type of mastectomy he recommended. From my readings on the FORCE Web site, I asked about the differences between skin-sparing, subcutaneous, and nipple-sparing mastectomies.

"Skin-sparing mastectomy, but not nipple-sparing is my recommendation," Dr. Anderson said. "Nipples are breast tissue and at risk of carcinoma."

He explained that *subcutaneous mastectomy* is a procedure that removes tissue through an incision under the breast, leaving the skin, nipple, and areola intact. The appeal of this procedure is the aesthetic result—after reconstruction there are no visible scars due to the incisions being hidden under the breasts; also, the patient retains her own nipples. However, working through an incision under the breast makes it impossible for the surgeon to remove as much tissue as the other procedures allow. In a *nipple-sparing mastectomy* the incision is made around the areola, which enables the surgeon to remove more tissue than in the subcutaneous procedure; however, the nipple and areola are still preserved, which increases cancer risk. *Skin-sparing mastectomy*—Dr. Anderson's choice—preserves the breast skin to hold and shape the reconstructed breasts, but entirely removes the nipples and areolas. Dr. Anderson's philosophy was to be as thorough as possible in removing at-risk tissue. This made sense to me. Why take this extreme measure without lowering your cancer odds as much as possible?

If I chose to undergo a skin-sparing mastectomy, the nipples would have to be reconstructed, and there were various methods to choose from. I would need to discuss that aspect as well as what type of reconstruction was best for me with a plastic surgeon. Dr. Anderson gave me the name of a colleague who he said did excellent work.

"I have one more question," I said. "I know that Myriad Labs performs all the BRCA tests in the country. Have you ever heard of them making a mistake? Is there a slim chance that my BRCA-positive test results could be wrong? Maybe I should take the test again."

"I've never heard of such an error. If you take the test again and receive negative results, your case would spur a national medical conference."

Kelly and I walked out of the office, oversaturated with information. We did not speak until we got into the elevator.

"I'm going to cancel my appointments with the other breast surgeons," I said.

"You're not going to do the surgery?" Kelly asked.

"I *am* going to do the surgery," I said with certainty. "Dr. Anderson is the right surgeon."

SIXTEEN

April–May 2005

Danielle had been listening to my deliberations for months without offering much of an opinion. She'd been processing all of the information along with me, and it was a lot to process. Considering that Danielle would have preferred to ignore our genetic legacy—and that I'd thrust the issue upon her—she'd been a remarkably patient sounding board. Once I'd actually made the decision to undergo a double mastectomy, however, she began to voice serious reservations.

"I just don't think you realize how you're going to feel when you wake up and your breasts are gone, Jessica. I don't think you appreciate how traumatic that will be."

"You're right, I can't imagine how I will feel. But it's the lesser of two evils. I'll be more traumatized if I wake up with cancer."

My mind was made up, so Dani insisted on accompanying me to meet Dr. Ward, the plastic surgeon Dr. Anderson had recommended. Danielle felt a responsibility to oversee the aesthetic aspect of this endeavor now that our mother was gone. If I was going to do it, she felt I'd better have a surgeon who did fastidious work and she didn't trust me to judge. There was merit to this. I could analyze a play, book, or film with expertise, but I glazed over when it came to seeing to matters of physical beauty that were instinctive to my mother and Danielle. I knew what I liked in a general way, but my vision was selective. I could not tell you about the cut of a dress or the shape of a coat, even if I wore it every day. I found most of my close girlfriends beautiful and could note and admire qualities that appealed to me, like a lovely complexion or long eyelashes, yet I never noticed when a friend gained some weight, nor did I recognize when women had nose jobs or boob jobs unless the results were Hollywood extreme. I probably wouldn't think to ask questions about breast reconstruction that were obvious to Danielle. Already, Dani had asked me things like "Would you want round or tear-drop shaped implants? High or low profile?" and I'd just stare blankly.

Dani and I were ushered into the plastic surgeon's office and Dr. Ward stood to greet us. His appearance was slick and Botoxed, and I instantly disliked him. He never looked me in the eye, and he talked fast and with manufactured enthusiasm. Before Danielle or I could get a word in, he steered us to seats and announced he'd be making a presentation. Dr. Ward flipped a switch that activated a slide show of reconstructed breasts and launched into a monologue. I found it hard to comprehend what he was saying because there was no feeling or natural inflection behind the words—he was motoring through to the end of his spiel. Pairs of breasts in different shapes and sizes flashed before us—the images were cropped above the belly button and below the neck. It reminded me of one of those subliminal scientific experiments. Twice Dani and I tried to ask questions and he shut us down like a put-upon schoolteacher, admonishing us to wait until he was finished. His manner offended me. Yet even as I realized how much I disliked this man, I had to admit the breasts on the slide show looked pretty and real. The reconstructed nipples were most impressive—no one would have guessed they were inauthentic. The only obvious imperfections were the mastectomy scars, which were pronounced on some of the breasts and less so on others.

Finally, the presentation ended, and Dr. Ward allowed a few questions. I asked what sort of reconstruction he would recommend for me. He glanced at my body and said, "Implants. You don't have enough fat for a TRAM flap." Danielle asked about the safety of silicone versus saline implants and he waved his hand dismissively, cutting her off with "Unquestionably silicone. All of that about the 'dangers of silicone' is rubbish. Saline implants look and feel like water balloons."

I mentioned that I'd always wished I'd had smaller breasts and wanted to take this opportunity to downsize. "I'd like to be a B-cup," I said.

"Oh no!" Dr. Ward replied. "You're an attractive, large-breasted girl—you can't go with anything smaller than a C."

"But that's not what I want," I replied.

"You don't have to worry about that now. Trust me, I'll make you beautiful. I guarantee you'll look better than when you started." This did not sit well with me. I had a strong feeling that Dr. Ward's idea of beauty was not mine.

Last, I brought up the slight rippling I had noticed on Suzy's reconstruction. For the first time, the plastic surgeon looked me straight in the eye.

"If you ever repeat this to anyone, I will deny it. But I recommend that you do not use Dr. Anderson as a breast surgeon."

"But Dr. Anderson sent us to you," I said. "What would make you say that?"

Dr. Ward gazed at me from under his frozen forehead as if we were co-conspirators. "Dr. Anderson is too aggressive—he scrapes out every bit of breast tissue and leaves me nothing to work with. If there's no breast tissue left to cushion the implant, it's impossible to get a good cosmetic result and there will be rippling. I suggest Dr. Deborah Vogal. She's much more sensitive to . . . shall we say, a woman's needs."

"As I understand it, the entire *purpose* of a prophylactic mastectomy is to remove as much breast tissue as possible. I'm taking this radical measure to avoid getting sick—the more breast tissue that remains, the higher the risk of cancer."

The doctor broke into a condescending smile. "So, your risk will be reduced by eighty or eighty-five percent instead of ninety. But your new breasts will look fantastic."

I left the office shaking, indignant. Should I call Dr. Anderson and tell him? Should I post a warning to women on the FORCE Web site to watch out for this creep? I felt Dr. Ward was not only unethical but dangerous. Danielle, the connoisseur of beauty, wholeheartedly agreed.

That night, I repeated the story to a friend, who said, "You're in Hollywood, what do you expect? If I were you, I'd have my breasts done in New York."

THOUGH THE INTERVIEW was still a month away, Courtney, the producer from *Nightline,* called me at work to say she was sending a local cameraman over to my office at *Gilmore Girls.* They needed some footage of me in my "natural environment."

"He'll be there Thursday," she said.

I hung up and tore into Rebecca's office.

"Thursday?" Rebecca asked. "That's only three days from now!"

"I know! What do I wear? What about makeup? And my office—what about my office?"

On my first writing job, I'd heard the superstition that a television writer should never decorate her office, because as soon as you got too comfortable the show would invariably be canceled or you would be fired or the guild would launch a strike. I'd always followed this rule, and it hadn't been uncommon on my former writing staffs. But Amy's decorating excesses at *Gilmore Girls* seemed to trump the superstition, because all the other writers had decked out their offices, exhibiting individual creative flair. In this context, my bare office was a sad, sorry, empty shell.

"We've got a lot of work to do," said Rebecca.

Rebecca was kind of a hybrid of me and Danielle. She and Dani looked somewhat alike—both head-turners, the same height, with long blond hair. Danielle had our mother's talents for design, yet she'd also been a math major at the University of Pennsylvania. Rebecca's parents are scientists—her father is a Harvard astrophysicist—and she'd inherited those mental faculties. Rebecca shared my love of literature, film, and art (we constantly traded books, had reading dates, and could spend hours debating the merits of Leni Riefenstahl or Truman Capote). She also had Danielle's gift of style, though Rebecca's taste was much more theatrical. If Danielle was the contractor of my breast reconstruction, Rebecca was the artistic director of the *Nightline* production.

With only a couple of weeks left to the television season, the final scripts had already been written and there was little work to do, which meant that Rebecca and I had lots of free time to go shopping. I drove us to Beverly Hills, which was an event in itself.

Apparently, I'm a terrible, reckless driver, but on my own I'm blissfully unaware of the fact. It's only when I have a passenger that the subject comes to light, and Rebecca was always my most miserable passenger. "Jess, you're going to great lengths not to die of cancer!" she shrieked. "Can you put a little more effort into not killing us in a car crash?!"

Rebecca swept through Barneys, choosing dresses, telling me what to try on and in what order, while I followed in her wake. Midway through the pile, I modeled a dusty-rose-colored dress and Rebecca declared, "That is what you *must* wear during the actual interview. It's elegant, it's sophisticated, it's *perfect*."

"Okay. With what shoes?"

"I would say tall, heeled brown boots."

Off we went to the shoe department. Rebecca made a beeline to a pair that cost half a month's rent, but we were manic, on a spree, and money was no object. The budget gods would wreak their vengeance later.

"I believe we're all out of this boot," the salesman said. "We haven't ordered more because it's a winter shoe. It's out of season. I doubt you'll find it anywhere." Suddenly, these boots were of dire importance to me—all of my anxiety over the breast cancer gene, my love life, my ticking clock was channeled into the compulsive need for this very specific pair of Jimmy Choos.

"You just have to have them," I said. "Will you check in the back?"

"I'll check," he said doubtfully.

And then a miracle occurred on the first floor of Barneys: The salesman emerged from the stockroom gingerly carrying a long, shiny box as if it contained two dozen long-stemmed roses.

"I can't believe it," he said with amazement. "There was one pair left and they're in your size."

"The ghost of my dead mother sent them to me!" I exclaimed like a raving lunatic. "She would insist on chocolate brown Jimmy Choos. Thank you, Mom!" I directed to the ceiling. Rebecca was doubled over, laughing at my madness and the madness of the situation. The irony was not lost on either of us that we were dressing me up like a doll to go on national television and talk about my plans to remove my breasts. Why be pious about the subject when we could turn it into a party? Why treat the interview like it was funereal when we could celebrate it as a joyful theatrical event? There were many layers of homage to my mother at play. After witnessing the disease ravage her, I would sacrifice what were arguably the most feminine parts of my body to prevent cancer. I would follow in her footsteps, emulate her fierce battle for life by offering up the beauty of my natural body in exchange for my life. Yet I could still wear Jimmy Choo boots (on occasion) and retain my inner and outer beauty and exuberance.

The day before the *Nightline* cameraman was due at *Gilmore Girls,* I loaded my car with pillows, fabric, and artwork—the raw materials for reinventing my office. I'd looted my apartment, ripped the framed photography off the walls, borrowed the white marble reclining Buddha from my entryway.

Bill Prady, the co-executive producer on the show, walked by and saw me and Rebecca standing on chairs, laughing and bantering as we hammered nails into the wall. "We have three weeks left of work and you're decorating *now?*"

"A crew from *Nightline* will be here tomorrow—we're making this place camera-ready," Rebecca exclaimed.

"You want everything to look good for the cameras?" Bill asked. "To help you out, I'll call Robert Downey Jr. and ask him to play me for the afternoon."

The next morning, the camera guy from *Nightline* shot some

footage of me typing at my desk, then he followed me and Rebecca to the writers' room and the set. He rigged a camera to the golf cart and set us free. We drove around the lot, babbling about any subject that came to mind—safaris in Africa, the photographer Lee Friedlander, Tasmanian devils—as people stared quizzically at the two girls on the loose in a golf cart with a movie camera aimed at them. Of course, when the show finally aired, they used ten seconds of footage from that day. My stylishly decorated office was never seen, and our carefully chosen outfits were merely glimpsed. But that had never really been the point. I was getting attention from a news show because of grave matters—my mother had died and I had inherited the gene that had caused her death. Rebecca's friendship helped me retain a certain joie de vivre. We were turning the proverbial lemons into lemonade. At a time when I could have been weighted down with depression, I felt alive and full of joy.

BY NOW, I was addicted to the FORCE Web site. I spent hours on it every day. Because I hated the Hollywood plastic surgeon, I'd decided that everything he'd told me was suspect. He'd recommended silicone implants and had insisted they were safe; I investigated his claims on the FORCE message boards. In this instance, Dr. Ward had not been wrong. I learned that the FDA was about to approve the availability of silicone implants for breast augmentation (elective boob jobs), lifting a fourteen-year ban. (Silicone had always remained available for women who required reconstruction for breast-cancer-related issues, which included prophylactic mastectomy due to BRCA mutations.) Extensive studies had examined whether silicone gel-filled implants were associated with connective tissue or autoimmune diseases and concluded there was no evidence of either. However, I learned on FORCE that silicone implants do not last a lifetime. Women with silicone implants would probably need to replace them at least once. Rupturing of the implants is most often silent; an MRI would be required to determine if rupture had occurred. Some people suggested replacing the implants every ten years, to be safe.

I didn't like the idea of having to have breast surgery every ten years. Maybe using my own body tissue was a better option. I read that the use of your own soft, warm, living tissue re-created breasts that feel extremely natural and would last for life. It was true that I didn't have enough stomach fat to make two new breasts, but a GAP (gluteal artery perforator) flap using tissue from the tush and performed by microsurgeons was apparently an option. There was a medical center in New Orleans where two doctors had perfected this technique and were able to make breasts from your buttocks no matter how slim you were. Many women on FORCE had flown to New Orleans for this procedure and were thrilled with the results. In a crazy small-world coincidence, my lawyer's nephew turned out to be one of the two pioneers of this microsurgical perforator flap method in New Orleans. We spoke on the phone. The surgeon said he'd read my Op-Ed piece and had been wanting to find a way to get in touch with me. He explained the benefits of his method. My new breasts would feel and act like normal breasts. They would change in volume as my normal weight fluctuated. We could do mastectomy and reconstruction all at once; if I chose to have implants, I would likely have two separate operations. (However, taking fat from my tush in addition to mastectomy and reconstruction would require an extremely long surgery and additional scars on my behind.) I was hesitant about the idea of having major surgery in New Orleans. This would require staying in a hotel in a remote city after being released from the hospital. I'd have to transplant my dad and sister; none of my friends would be around to visit or relieve them. But it was my next question that was the deciding factor. I asked the surgeon if my new breasts would sag as the years went on like real breasts do. He said yes. Suddenly, I liked the idea of implants again. Breasts that never sag and never require a bra? To me, that was the unexpected silver lining of this ordeal.

THE *GILMORE GIRLS* season came to a close. On the last day of work I wished everyone a happy hiatus, skipped out on the wrap party, and waved good-bye to Joe the security guard as I drove off the lot and headed for the airport. I caught a red-eye to New York, where I planned to spend two days hanging out with friends before flying to D.C. for the *Nightline* interview. I was run-down from stress and emerged from the plane the next morning with a pounding head, watery eyes, and a stuffy nose. I got sicker as the day wore on. Kay had a party for us to attend that night and would not hear of my canceling. "Some orange juice and vodka will do the trick," she said. The party was for the World Voices Festival of International Literature sponsored by PEN, and I'd been looking forward to it. I was excited to be out of Hollywood and agreed that a night out with Kay among the New York literati would be a far better tonic than sleep. Kay came over to fetch me and was wearing a striking turquoise dress. I rifled through the closet, past my old reliable dresses, and pulled out a robin's-egg-blue, Grecian frock that I rarely wore because of its deep neckline. "I might as well give my breasts a last hurrah," I offered. I downed Sudafed, stuffed my coat pockets with Kleenex, and we were off.

Heads turned as Kay and I entered the dimly lit bar in our conspicuous blue dresses. I noted instantly that all the other women in the room were dressed in black. Apparently, it was the female intelligentsia's uniform. The one other woman wearing colorful, sexy, eye-catching garb was the model Padma Lakshmi, Salman Rushdie's then-wife. I had a twinge of regret over my outfit, wishing I could blend in with the women in black, but there was nothing to be done, so I pushed the feeling down. "Kay, where's that orange juice and vodka?"

Within minutes, Padma glided across the room to strike up conversation with Kay. They'd never met, but both were standouts in the crowd—tall and unapologetic beauties. Birds of a feather, I thought. I was chatting with a young journalist named Ann when a German woman in her late forties with a curtain of blond hair and a martini spun around from the bar. She looked me up and down with dramatic flair, lingering for a moment on my cleavage. Then she pounced.

"That's *some* dress you're wearing."

The insult was so blatant I thought I must have misunderstood.

"Thank you."

"No. What I mean is that's *quite* a dress. When I'm getting ready to go out, I think about where I'm going and what might be *appropriate* to wear."

No mistake. The German dragon lady had called me a bimbo for sport. Several onlookers were now gaping. After a moment of shock, rage surged through me. My nose was runny, my head was still pounding its reminder that I hadn't slept for days, but this bitchy attack was the last straw. I locked eyes with the German.

"I'm thirty-four years old and I'm about to undergo a double mastectomy because I tested positive for the BRCA genetic mutation. I'm in the prime of my life and my body's still intact, so I figured I might as well enjoy it while I can—*that's* why I wore this dress. And I'm looking for someone to father my child because I also need my ovaries removed, so if anyone comes to mind, let me know."

The woman fell into stunned silence, as another woman chimed in, "You didn't happen to write a recent Op-Ed piece, did you?"

"Yes," I said, thrilled at this extra bit of vindication.

"I'm Sarah," she introduced herself. "I sent that article to many people."

"I read it, too!" Ann the journalist added.

"I also have cancer in my family," Sarah said. "I've thought about you a lot. . . . How are you doing?"

Sarah and Ann engaged me in conversation about cancer prevention as the villain deflated on her bar stool. Sarah embraced me and took my phone number, exclaiming that she was going to work on finding me a man.

TWO DAYS LATER, I was sitting in a chair opposite Cokie Roberts on the small set of a television studio. The lights were bright, the walls draped with heavy brown fabric, the cameras rolling. I'd flown in the night before and knocked myself out with NyQuil, had been escorted from the hotel to the *Nightline* offices bright and early, and the next thing I knew we were mid-interview. It had happened so fast, there hadn't been time to get nervous.

The segment would be narrated by Ted Koppel. The piece was titled "Mother and Daughter" and aired on May 6, 2005, right before Mother's Day. I heard Koppel's introduction for the first time while watching the show:

Tonight is the story of a young woman who learns what she's
inherited from her mother, a predisposition to cancer, and

the excruciating choices she learns how to make. The world
is probably more or less evenly divided between those of us
who would like to know what lies in the future and those who
would not. If, for example, you could know the date on which,
and circumstances under which, you were going to die, would
you want to know? Knowing would give you the opportunity
to plan. But likely as not, you would also worry. What if
knowledge also carried with it the opportunity to change the
future? And that, in one very important respect, is what this
program is about tonight.

Because Cokie Roberts was my friend Liza's mother-in-law,
she was protective of me; I felt safe and assured of the fact that
the interview would be tasteful. That said, Cokie's questions were
provocative (which, of course, makes for good television). Early
on, she asked me why I wouldn't just opt to get breast cancer and
treat it. "Every day there are more treatment options, more thera-
pies available for breast cancer. Many of us are walking around
having had breast cancer. . . ."

This would turn out to be the most controversial moment of
the interview. After the show aired, many people would tell me
the question had offended them. One of my doctors found it to be
outrageous. She said, "There is no guarantee that breast cancer is
'curable.' Cancer is a wild card, it doesn't play by the normal rules.
Once you've had cancer, you will always live with the burden that
it may return. Whether the cancer has been 'cured' is a conclusion that can only be made in retrospect." As I continued to meet
people whose lives had been touched by cancer, I found there to
be a clear split. Those who had witnessed relatives beat cancer,
or who had beaten cancer themselves, often tended to view it as
something manageable, something you get through. Others, like

me, who had witnessed the death grip of cancer, tended to have a much darker perspective.

My answer to Cokie's question:

I spoke to many oncologists around the country, one of whom was your doctor, and I think it was she who told me it really is a personal choice; it's a question of your tolerance for fighting breast cancer. MRIs now are much more sophisticated than mammograms were. It's likely that in my case they could catch cancer quite early. My answer is that having watched my mother die a brutal, horrific death—to me, cancer is the worst thing in the world, I don't want to gamble with it. I don't want to gamble that maybe we'll catch it early enough. After going through a long, long process I came to the decision that I would do anything I needed to do to prevent it in the first place.

Later in the interview, Cokie referred to my decision to undergo a prophylactic mastectomy and asked, "Do you find that there are people who think that you're crazy?"

"Yes," I replied.

Though my reaction was composed, the question rattled me. *Crazy* is a strong word. Did Cokie Roberts think I was crazy? Would the millions of *Nightline* viewers now think I was crazy? *Was* I crazy? By this point, I'd spoken with enough doctors to feel assured that a BRCA-positive woman opting for a preventive mastectomy was not a woman overreacting. Still, the question reminded me of how radical the surgery seemed to most people.

"What do they say?"

"Well, to my face they don't tell me that they think that I'm crazy. But you get the sense people are judgmental, and they feel that maybe I'm being melodramatic or jumping the gun, and 'Why can't she just do screening? Is that extreme really necessary?' And I understand, I felt the same way at first."

The most gratifying aspect of the interview was how much time I was allowed to talk about my mother. In the produced segment, photos of my mom filled the screen as I described her life and death. It was a great gift for me to honor my mother in such a public way.

I was most embarrassed by the questions about my personal life. I had to explain that I was single and wanted children and needed to find a way to have them before the age of forty, when I would have my ovaries removed.

"Talk about pressure!" Cokie said. "I mean the biological clock ticks, but it's ticking very loud."

"Yes, that is very upsetting and distressing to me. . . . But I've come to peace with the mastectomy and I'm also at peace with the idea of having a child or two in the next five years, and if I have to do it on my own, I will do it on my own. And if the right person comes along, God bless him. . . ." (I buried my head in my hands with embarrassment over that line when I saw it on TV. *God bless him?* Where did that come from?) "But I'm going to do whatever I need to do."

At some point Cokie remarked, "You say all of that, but it's all very brave." That's how I felt about the interview as a whole. I was giving all of the brave answers and acting confident that the things I said would come to pass. I would have the mastectomy; it would be better than cancer; a man of substance would choose to be with me in spite of it; in the event that the man did not materialize in time, I would have children on my own, after which I would remove my ovaries. Just as I had calmly told Ron Schwary that I would dash off a screenplay adaptation, while in reality I panicked, I was now calmly announcing to the world that I would take these actions and all would be well, while inside I was frantic. I had no idea whether all would be well or if I would fall apart. The only operation I'd ever had was the removal of my wisdom teeth. My romantic pickiness had precluded my finding a partner without the complication of a cancer gene. I'd never even had my own pet—how exactly would I manage if I had to have a child without a partner? However, this approach had been the pattern in my life. I'd set a courageous goal for myself, act as if I could do it, and either sink or swim. Usually, I managed at least to tread water.

I was almost eerily calm throughout the taping of the interview. My formidable neuroses were kind enough to stay asleep that day. They woke up with a vengeance on May 6, the night the segment was to air, and raged like an angry bear. A small group of my closest friends in New York met me at a restaurant called Rain on the Upper West Side before we were to head over to Gillian's apartment for the *Nightline* viewing. While en route to dinner, I made the taxi driver pull over because I thought I was going to throw up. Once at the restaurant, I spent a total of two minutes at the table; my nausea had transformed into a ferocious stomachache and I could not leave the bathroom stall. Over the next hour, my girlfriends took turns traipsing down the stairs to the ladies' room to check on me. "Jess, are you in there? Should we order the food to go? Should we leave and take you to the apartment?"

"Oh no, you guys go ahead and enjoy dinner. . . ." I said feebly. "I'm too ill to relocate. . . ." I spent the meal in the restroom, and then was transported to Gillian's. After I was planted on her sofa, my neuroses took on a new manifestation: Tension seized my upper body and I could no longer turn my head right or left.

"Don't get me wrong, I'm *grateful* that my body decided to

break down during the *viewing* of the interview rather than the *taping,* but what the hell is going on with me?" I cried, illustrating my Frankenstein stiffness to the amusement of all.

"So you're about to appear on national television and tell millions of people you're going to remove your breasts," Jonathan teased. "What's all the fuss about?"

As with the article, the interview elicited an outpouring of passionate responses representing both sides of the argument—to know or not to know, to act or not to act. Many people posted letters to me on a Web site called Genetics, Cancer and Prophylaxis. Several women supported my decision and shared their own stories. Others were vehemently opposed to my choosing mastectomy.

One woman with stage IV inflammatory breast cancer that had metastasized to her lungs, liver, and chest wall wrote: "To Jessica—Don't jump the gun. I did chemo twice, radiation, and had a modified radical mastectomy. It's not so bad. I had four and a half years of remission before relapse. During that time, I raised my children, went back to school, earned a degree, changed careers, fell in love, and cherished every moment. I have taken Maitake mushroom supplements and Noni juice since first being diagnosed. Try the natural stuff first, have a relationship, have your children, and face cancer IF it comes."

Another woman: "To Jessica—I just finished hearing you on *Nightline* and am stunned by your decision. Please take a very close look at glyconutrients as they are vital to the proper function of our cells. . . ."

One man posted: "Jessica, it is not my place to tell you not to have the surgery you've chosen, but life is strange, you could be hit by a bus a week after surgery, and put yourself through all this for naught! And a cure, or a better test, or treatment could be discovered next week! Sometimes by being too rational and too cautious we hurt ourselves in the process. I believe you will find love, children, and all the dreams you mentioned regardless of your choice, but at least give it as long as you can before; I'd take healthy living and faith in God over such drastic prophylactic protection any day. . . ."

One young guy who'd watched the piece told a friend of mine that prophylactic mastectomy, to him, was "the equivalent of being castrated."

The women of the FORCE Web site had quite a lot to say about the *Nightline* segment. Though FORCE had become a consistent presence in my life, I was still a silent reader. I'd never posted a question or comment or otherwise identified myself to the community. Several women posted warm responses to my interview while lamenting the fact that I apparently didn't know about FORCE. Others were not as kind. One woman was incensed that I had not extolled the merits of genetic counseling on television. She also felt the manner in which I'd found out about my BRCA status was like a "Three Stooges act" (not an inaccurate description, and an unwitting nod to my grandmother Harriette). She called me uneducated on BRCA issues and lamented that some Hollywood girl with connections would be the spokeswoman for this topic rather than someone qualified like FORCE's leader, Sue Friedman.

I sent in my first post to FORCE. I identified myself and said I'd been reading the Web site obsessively for months and thought FORCE an amazing resource and Sue Friedman heroic. I explained that in a thirty-minute television segment, the producers had to pick and choose what to use from an interview. I'd spoken at

length about genetic counseling, health insurance, and other important issues. All of this had been cut in the editing process.

Once I made my debut online, the letters poured in. So many
FORCE women wrote to say they'd watched the piece, had deeply
identified with the pain over losing a loved one to cancer, and
shared the same genetic struggles. They wrote of their personal
histories. The woman who'd written the angry note apologized and
removed sections of her previous post. Many expressed how
stunned they had been by Cokie Roberts's suggestion that getting
cancer was an option. One wrote:

"Cancer of any kind should not be considered an option, but a
horrific, life-changing event, occurring without our consent. I'm
currently in treatment and have watched my mom and five of her
siblings suffer through their treatments, some successfully, some
not. Bravo to you, Jessica, for choosing NOT to take the risk/op-
tion of cancer."

Another: "I have always liked Cokie Roberts—I know she is
a cancer survivor as well—but did she suggest that an option for
you would be to actually get breast cancer? I realize that there
are many women who are living well after breast cancer but your
answer was spot on—it is not an option and I was glad you said
what you did. As someone who is living with cancer, I was proud
of you."

Though Jason and I had not been romantically involved since
the time of the Writers Guild seminar, we were still close. Neither
of us had started seeing anyone else, and getting back together had
always hung in the air as a possibility. He had viewed the *Nightline*
segment from his apartment in Los Angeles and exclaimed with
admiration how poised I'd been. It had amazed him.

"You were great," he said. "But I didn't recognize you."

"What do you mean?"

"You were so strong, so together, so certain. You were a *woman*. Nothing like the girl I know."

That was the final moment of epiphany. I'd met Jason while in distress and he'd swept in as the knight. That was the dynamic that had remained between us. He was a caretaker who drew out my helpless, kittenish side, not the part of me I strove to embody—my articulate, capable self.

I'd always known that if I remained in Los Angeles for the surgery, Jason would be by my side, and the thought was comforting and reassuring. I gathered my courage and made a decision: I would move back to New York and have the surgery on the East Coast. It was time for us both, finally, to move on, and for me to brave this ordeal by myself.

SEVENTEEN

June 2005

packed up my Hollywood apartment and braced myself to face the trials ahead without a significant other.

And yet. Two days before leaving for New York, I agreed to go on a blind date. A tiny optimistic voice within me whispered that I wouldn't *really* have to go through this without a man who loved me. I planned to schedule the surgery for early September, which left a whole luxurious summer in which to fall in love. Surely, God or fate or karma would even out all my misfortune by sending me the right partner before my body underwent irrevocable transformation?

Over lunch with my attorney, I had discussed my pending operation and lamented the state of my love life, which spurred her to set me up with a successful independent film director. Luis Porta and I talked for a few minutes on the phone to establish the time and place of our date. He asked what I was working on, and I said I was about to take some time off from television writing to live in New York and maybe write a book. "What's the book about?" My answer was vague, though I alluded to an article I'd written that would serve as the launching point.

At the restaurant, over my first sip of wine, Luis said, "So I read your article." I swallowed slowly, careful not to choke. This was the precise scenario I'd imagined with horror. "After we hung up the other night, I Googled you. That's a pretty rough situation."

I was startled by this—it felt like trespassing, but why did it? After all, I'd Googled him, too. I tried to make light of it.

"Well, at least living in the Internet age spares us the awkwardness of first-date questions, right? You do your homework and then cut right to the chase at dinner. . . ."

Luis was a hipster with a low-key, quiet persona. He asked me questions and listened while nodding in empathy. It was hard to tell whether he was truly sensitive or faux sensitive, but I continued refilling my glass with wine and chose to believe the former. Luis told me about his recent heartbreak—the ugly end of his relationship with another emerging indie-film director. (I had already read about this online. I'd even looked up her photo.) As the night progressed, I discovered I liked his taste in films. I liked his tranquil manner. I liked *him*.

"I was sort of dreading this blind date. . . . I thought about canceling it," I said, meeting his gaze. "I'm so glad I didn't."

Luis responded in kind. I was too blurry with wine to remember the exact words, but the sentiment appeared to be mutual. We did not kiss good night, but it was a warm parting. I felt sure we would go out again.

The next day Luis left a message on my machine to give him a call. "He called right away!" I told Kay. "I'm so happy!" Within minutes I left a message for him suggesting another date before I took off for New York. That afternoon while I was out, he called back:

"Hey, Jessica, it's Luis. I'm a very straightforward person, so I'm going to be honest with you. It sounds like you're going through some heavy stuff right now, and I'm not really up for that. So, it was nice meeting you. And, uh, good luck."

Of course. Why would a man with options *choose* to get involved with me now? Luis's reaction had confirmed my fears. I closed up my Hollywood home with a heavy heart and flew to New York.

DR. JULIA SMITH is a tall, handsome woman with silver gray hair and warmth that fills a room. Her office is at the NYU hospital, where my mother had been treated and where I planned to have my surgeries. Dr. Smith is the director of breast cancer screening and prevention at the NYU Cancer Institute and the director of the Lynn Cohen Breast Cancer Prevention Care Program. It took about ten seconds to recognize that she was extraordinary. She was doctor, scientist, mentor, philosopher, and earth mother wrapped up in one.

Dr. Smith helps high-risk women take action *before* they get cancer. She counsels women about the benefits and drawbacks of learning their BRCA status before they've been tested, and then advises them about their options after they've been tested. By the time I met Dr. Smith, I knew my BRCA status and had already made the decision to undergo surgery. What I needed was reassurance and support. During our first appointment, Dr. Smith examined me, and then we spent two hours talking in her office. Her attention was rapt and complete as I told her my history.

"Once cancer strikes, the world changes," she said. "The axis of the planet shifts and you will never experience it the same way again. Listening to my cancer patients describe how they feel is strikingly similar to how people describe feeling after 9/11. The threat of a terrorist attack had always been there, had always been the same. However, people's understanding and awareness of it changed after 9/11. Cancer is like a terrorist attack from within. You're going along, doing your thing, you know the threat of cancer exists theoretically, but you're not thinking about it, it's not coloring your life. After it strikes, even if it is 'cured,' you will always be on red alert, waiting for it to return."

While Dr. Smith acknowledged that prophylactic surgery was not right for everyone, there was no question that she endorsed my decision. During our first meeting and throughout the summer, whenever I grew frightened or doubtful, she continued to affirm that I was doing the right thing.

"I've made up my mind," I said that first day. "But I do lie awake some nights worrying that I'm being overzealous. Friends keep reminding me that I don't have to have the operation right now . . . that I could wait a few years. . . ."

"Remember that this surgery is noninvasive, Jessica. It's *external*. If you wait until you get breast cancer, you will do the mastectomy anyway and then you'll likely have to put toxins into your body—chemotherapy, tamoxifen. Plus, we will never know for sure that the cancer is gone. From that point on, we will have to be worried about your life."

My dad had persuaded me to take the BRCA test a second time, to be absolutely certain that the results were correct. The test cost three thousand dollars and insurance would not pay for it twice, so my father had written me a check on the spot. If I was going to go forward with mastectomy, he insisted that we know—without a shadow of a doubt—that I carried the mutant gene. I'd told him what Dr. Anderson had said: That kind of mistake would be such an anomaly it would spur a national medical conference.

"So let them have their conference," he said. "I've been trying malpractice cases for over forty years. Labs make mistakes."

Dr. Smith brought me back into the exam room and drew my blood for the second BRCA test. I had a moment of giddiness, imagining the results coming back negative. How crazy and wonderful would it be if this nightmare was all just a lab mix-up?

I made an appointment to see Dr. Smith again in two weeks to get the results.

In the subway on my way to see Dr. Smith for the second time, I indulged my fantasy of receiving negative results. I imagined her incredulous expression as she told me about this unprecedented occurrence. She'd say it was a one-in-a-million incident, like a hospital sending a new mother home with the wrong baby. The new results would show with certainty that I was negative. I was free to go, resume my normal life, run out of the hospital into the sunshine and never look back.

"Your test came back positive, Jessica," Dr. Smith said as I walked into her office. I sat down, deflated. "The results are identical to the first. You have the 187delAG genetic variant. It's one of three founder mutations, and it's the variant most common among Ashkenazi Jewish women."

Though I knew it was irrational, I felt surprised all over again. Like my mother, I was an optimist until the bitter end.

Now that all doubt of my genetic status had been removed, we returned to the matter at hand—planning my operations. I had decided that I wanted to use my mother's breast surgeon, Dr. Daniel Roses, for the mastectomy, and had already scheduled an appointment to see him. Dr. Smith recommended that I meet with the plastic surgeon Dr. Miyhe Choi for the reconstruction.

"Oh, there's a young woman I want you to meet," Dr. Smith added, as I headed toward the elevators. "Her name is Donna. She's just about made the decision to schedule her preventive mastectomy. You two have a lot in common."

Later that week I scheduled an appointment with Dr. Choi. Danielle had also moved back to New York—to move in with Bruce—and accompanied me. Dr. Choi was petite and beautiful. Her many years of practice indicated she was older than I was, though she could have been mistaken for a medical student. The three of us sat in her office while Danielle and I recounted our mother's history and my subsequent BRCA testing. Dr. Choi quietly added that she'd also lost her mother to cancer and surprised us (and herself) by welling up with tears. The moment passed quickly, and, though subtle, it was evident that Dr. Choi felt embarrassed over letting her guard down in front of patients, but I loved her for it.

Dr. Choi agreed that we should re-create breasts with implants. She said I did not have enough fat or skin on my stomach to create two breasts of any size. Though she could create flaps through microsurgery from my buttocks, she felt the scars would be too deforming. For some patients, she preferred autologous reconstruction (using body tissue from donor sites) because there are advantages to using your own body tissue rather than inserting foreign objects. Implants require monitoring, and on occasion, scar tissue will form around them, which causes hardening of the new breasts, whereas body tissue creates a soft, natural feel. On the other hand, autologous reconstruction requires extensive surgery and a far more difficult recovery. Dr. Choi didn't feel that my body type was optimal for flaps; in addition she didn't think I should undergo more extensive procedures than necessary.

Dr. Choi talked us through the mastectomy and reconstruction process. After Dr. Roses removed the breast tissue during the mastectomy, Dr. Choi would be called into the OR to put "tissue expanders" under my pectoralis major chest muscle that would form a pocket. The skin and muscle had to be stretched gradually over the course of a couple months by the expanders to make room for implants. She would fill the expanders with saline during the initial procedure so that I would never be fully flat-chested. When I woke up from the operation, I would have slight breast mounds, equivalent to an A-cup. I'd spend about four days in the hospital and would have surgical drains attached to me for at least a week. Assuming the incisions were healing well, two or three weeks post-op I'd begin getting weekly "fills" at Dr. Choi's office—saline injections that would inflate the expanders. I could decide what size I wanted to be as we went along. Once I was happy with the size, we would do one final fill (it's necessary to overexpand to fit the desired implant size) and schedule my "exchange surgery." The first operation—the mastectomy—would take around three to four hours and would be the most difficult procedure. The exchange surgery would also be done under general anesthesia, but I wouldn't need to stay in the hospital overnight. The final surgery would be for nipple reconstruction. From beginning to end, the procedures would span five to six months.

I launched into my speech about how I wanted smaller breasts, how all these years of being a D-cup had driven me crazy. I wanted to wear slip dresses and tank tops with ease. I wanted to burn my vast collection of underwire minimizer harnesses. I no longer wanted to be a Russ Meyer supervixen! Dr. Choi laughed and said I could be any size I desired. I loved having a female plastic surgeon, because to me, the business of breast size was delicate and complicated. The last thing I needed was a male doctor bullying me with his ideals of feminine beauty.

Danielle and I asked questions about saline versus silicone. Dr. Choi said she felt confident in the safety of the newly manufactured silicone implants, though saline was the safest, most conservative route. The newer silicone implants were encased in thicker shells and ruptured far less often than the older models. Also, the consistency of the silicone was more cohesive and less likely to leak. She gave us samples of each to feel, and told me I had plenty of time to think about it.

"What about the new 'gummy bear' implants?" I asked. "I've read about them online."

Dr. Choi said they were being used mainly in Europe and had not yet been approved for use at N.Y.U. They were nicknamed "gummy bears" because they had the consistency of the candy and never leaked. But they were harder in feel than the silicone models she preferred.

"Do you have any photographs of your work . . . ?" I asked near the end of our meeting.

"Oh, yes!" Dr. Choi exclaimed. "Let me find them. . . ."

She foraged around on her computer for images. As we looked at them, Danielle nodded her approval. Dr. Choi's work was beautiful, and her manner was antithetical to the slick Hollywood doctor's schtick.

The next day, Danielle and I went to see Dr. Roses. He is an eminent, old-school, hard-boiled surgeon and a man of few words. As Liza Wherry had described in her letter, Dr. Roses showed uncharacteristic emotion when speaking of our mother. His eyes flickered with what could be called wistfulness as he referred to her as an extraordinary woman. He commended me on my intelligent decision to undergo prophylactic mastectomy and assured me of how rigorous he would be in removing my breast tissue. Like Dr. Anderson, he advocated a skin-sparing double mastectomy. His

secretary (and wife of many years) called Dr. Choi's office to
coordinate a date. The mastectomy was scheduled for September
12. Two months away.

I WAS LIVING in Harriette's Fifty-seventh Street apartment and
trying to work on that screenplay I'd been toting around in my
head and—like every other Hollywood writer—had never gotten
around to writing. I found myself falling into lethargy tinged with
depression, sleeping far more than typing. I spent many weekends
with my old friend and ex-boyfriend Jonathan and his wife, Alexandra, at their house in the Springs of East Hampton, which lifted
my spirits. Alexandra is a dark-haired beauty who had been a lesbian at Vassar and beyond. It wasn't until her midtwenties that she
shifted her romantic orientation to men and shortly thereafter met
Jonathan. Alexandra's ex-girlfriend Amy remained in her life as
her best friend. Amy and I were each other's counterparts in this
postmodern urban family: I was Jonathan's ex and best friend, and
she was Alex's. Jonathan and Amy had striking similarities—both
were sharp-witted, cerebral, funny Jews with enormous hearts.
When they were together, it required great effort to keep up with
their lightning-speed banter. Alexandra and I could be mistaken
for sisters and had similar sensibilities—we were both emotional,
effusive, girl's girls. (Jonathan and Amy would joke they had the
same taste in women—feminine, dark-haired, large-breasted Jew-
esses. Though soon enough—I enjoyed reminding them—I would
have small breasts and no longer be their type.) Amy and Jonathan formed their own singular friendship, as did Alexandra and I.
Since Amy and I were both single, we all joked that if only I were
into women, everything would fall into place. (A few years later

Alexandra would give birth to a baby boy and they would ask Amy to be the godmother, after which Jonathan would special-order a bib that read "My Mother Dated My Godmother, Beat That.") The other common denominator among the four of us was that all of our mothers had died. Jonathan's mother had committed suicide when he was six; Alexandra's mother had died of breast cancer when she was ten. Amy's mother had died of breast cancer one year before my mother died of ovarian cancer. This created a unique connection, a heightened empathy among us. When my mother was gravely ill, Jonathan and Alexandra called every day from their honeymoon. They began to refer to me as their "Mormon wife," though it would have been more accurate to call them my surrogate parents. There was something extremely comforting to me about being around Jonathan and Alexandra. I felt fully myself and most at ease. The only strain—and it was subtle—had to do with my pending mastectomy. Alexandra's mother (an Ashkenazi Jew) had been diagnosed with breast cancer in her early forties, which placed Alex in the high-risk category for a BRCA mutation. Alex was trying to get pregnant that summer and was not ready to face this threat. I had no wish to proselytize and didn't, but my upcoming surgery was an ever-present reminder that she too was at risk.

AT MY NEXT APPOINTMENT with Dr. Smith, I found a pretty young woman sitting in her office.

"Jessica, this is Donna—the woman I was telling you about. I scheduled overlapping appointments so you two could meet."

Dr. Smith left us alone in her office. As had happened with Suzy Hurley, Donna and I instantly fell into intimate conversation, losing all sense of time. An hour passed before Dr. Smith had to reclaim her office, at which point Donna and I scheduled a dinner date to continue our conversation later that week.

Donna Estreicher was born in 1971 on Staten Island. She was the youngest of three girls in a Jewish family and two years younger than I.

Donna's maternal grandmother died of ovarian cancer in her fifties, and her paternal grandmother died of ovarian cancer at age eighty-six. Donna's mom got breast cancer at fifty-eight. She'd been on hormone replacement therapy after menopause, which was thought to be the cause. The tumor was small and contained, so chemotherapy wasn't necessary—she had a lumpectomy and radiation. She never got very sick, and Donna's life was not much affected by her mother's cancer. She didn't experience it as terribly scary or life-threatening.

Five years later, in 2004, Donna's oldest sister, Beth, finished breast-feeding the last of her three kids and was unhappy with the state of her boobs—she felt they were flat and empty. Beth began interviewing plastic surgeons for a boob job. The third plastic surgeon she met discovered a lump. Just two months earlier she'd gone for a mammogram and had been given clean results. She was thirty-seven.

Beth immediately went to a breast surgeon, who discovered a second lump in the same breast. It was revealed to be an aggressive cancer. Because she had a family history and was so young, Beth was given the BRCA test. She tested positive for BRCA-1. Beth scheduled a double mastectomy and eight months later an oophorectomy. Her cancer was estrogen receptor (ER) negative. ER-negative tumors are less responsive to hormonal or biologic manipulation as they lack the targets for agents such as tamoxifen—meaning ER-negative cancer is more difficult to treat because

there are fewer nonsurgical options and it is more biologically aggressive. Because of the nature of her cancer, Beth was told she
had a 20 percent chance of recurrence even with mastectomy and
chemo.

Carolyn, the middle sister, was thirty-five with two kids and
took the BRCA test right away. She tested negative. Their parents
were tested, and surprisingly, the mutation was passed down from
their father.

Donna was thirty-two and single when Beth was diagnosed
with breast cancer. At the time, she resolved that she would never
take the BRCA test because she would never have a mastectomy.

Beth was very private about her experience with breast cancer,
so when she invited both sisters and their mom to join her for
a Young Survival Coalition weekend in Philadelphia, Donna was
overjoyed that Beth had reached out and included them. Donna
did not give any thought to how the weekend might affect her
emotionally.

One thousand women, at all different stages of breast cancer,
attended the conference. Some were currently undergoing treatment; others had been in remission for five years or more. Each
wore a Hawaiian lei around her neck to indicate how long she'd
been a survivor; every color represented a different length of time.
There were seminars on different topics throughout the day, and
the Estreichers attended whatever sessions interested Beth. They
went to many that focused on how destructive chemotherapy is
to the body. People spoke of how chemo had affected their mental capacities—what they called "chemo brain." Others described
symptoms like diminished libido and premature menopause. Donna
was traumatized by these lectures and left the weekend more
frightened of chemotherapy than of cancer.

After that weekend, Donna was an emotional wreck. She kept

thinking, "I'm a time bomb." She would dissolve into tears with no apparent provocation. Of the three sisters, Donna and Beth were the most similar—they looked alike, had the same mannerisms and temperaments. Donna felt sure she carried the mutation, but she still resisted taking the test.

One day on the bus, Donna had an epiphany—she described it as a "flash." "Wait a minute, why *can't* I get a mastectomy? Why not? Why have I written it off as a possibility?" She made an appointment to talk with Beth's breast surgeon and consider this further. Donna didn't want to take the BRCA test unless she was ready to take action.

Startlingly, upon examination, the surgeon felt a lump in Donna's breast. The doctor performed a needle biopsy immediately and the results were negative. Yet because of her family history, the surgeon recommended lumpectomy. This scare spurred Donna on to schedule the BRCA test. She resigned herself to having a mastectomy if she carried the mutation.

In April 2005, at age thirty-three, Donna received her positive results.

She had the lumpectomy anyway, because she needed more time to process this information before removing her breasts.

Now, in July 2005, Donna and I were sharing a bottle of wine in an Italian restaurant on the Upper East Side. We both confessed to being edgy and depressed in a large sense, though at the moment, we were reveling in each other's company. Like me, Donna was tormented over the fact that she was single. "It's hard enough to meet someone," she said. "Now I'm going to have a disfigured body?" She said that she had no interest in talking to anyone who had a prophylactic mastectomy and was married. As far as Donna was concerned, if someone already loved them, they were not in the same boat.

Donna took a sip of wine. "I guess I feel angry," she said. "It's almost like I've been told that I'm already sick, that I've already been diagnosed with cancer." When she went to parties and people casually asked, "How are you?" she felt unable to engage in mindless chitchat or act normally. She felt different from those carefree people, isolated. She was shrouded by her BRCA status.

I told her that I found I was short-tempered lately, too, and had no tolerance for most people. When my friend rattled on about her five-year-old son resisting sleep at bedtime and her insecurity over whether she'd chosen the right kindergarten, I felt disproportionately angry. The slightest thing could push me over the edge. But more often I just felt down. To me, September 12 was doomsday. Life as I knew it would be over. I'd never again be young and whole and free. As the summer wore on, I felt increasingly anxious about time running out.

Donna had scheduled her surgery for November—two months after mine—and she was also using Dr. Choi as her plastic surgeon. We discussed silicone versus saline implants. Donna had done more comprehensive research than I had on the topic—she'd read studies and learned about the different manufacturers. She felt reassured about the safety of silicone and said that if she had to go through all of this, she at least deserved to come out of it with the best possible aesthetic result. I agreed and admitted I'd opted for implants rather than flap reconstruction mainly because I didn't want my new breasts to sag. We segued into a mutual confession of the guilty pleasures of mastectomy: I said I was incredibly excited to have smaller boobs. She laughed because she was doing the opposite—Donna had the body of a ballerina and was delighted that she'd have large, sexy breasts. We agreed it was sort of cool that we would get to try on a different breast size each week during the expansion process as if it were a new dress.

How many women would get to have that experience? We discussed whether or not to have our sentinel nodes removed. The sentinel node is the first lymph node reached by metastasizing cancer cells. In a prophylactic mastectomy, it's presumed that the breast tissue does not yet have any cancer cells, but the removed breast tissue is sent to pathology to make sure of this. If the path report is clean and no cancer is present, there's no need to check lymph nodes. However, if cancer is found, the surgeon must determine whether or not it has spread to the nodes. Removing the sentinel node in advance is a safety guard—if it's not removed and cancer is found in the tissue, another surgery will be required. However, removing the sentinel node can cause lymphedema—a condition that can result in swelling of the arm. There is no medical consensus about whether to remove the sentinel node during prophylactic mastectomy—it's another instance of patients having to make a decision for themselves. Donna and I concluded that we would gamble that we were cancer-free and not have the node removed. We drank more wine and laughed again at the fact that we were trading boobs—I wanted hers and she wanted mine—and at how we'd been given the unique opportunity to re-create our bodies in a way that matched our inner vision of ourselves. What an extraordinary occurrence.

If the couple at the next table, or the waiter, or the single guy at the bar had been asked what the two young women at the table by the window were talking about so passionately, the answer might have been men or sex or the latest episode of *The Sopranos*. Not a soul could have imagined we were talking about how we would soon be having our breasts surgically removed.

EIGHTEEN

August 2005

The weeks were moving swiftly. It was becoming clear that I was not going to meet someone before the operation. This reality drew me deeper into depression. Somehow I'd believed that magic was going to occur over the summer, that my life and love would be settled before the surgery.

"I bet you're going to fall in love with your surgeon," Rebecca had said. "It's going to be some crazy story like that."

"Considering my breast surgeon is a man in his sixties and my plastic surgeon is a young Asian woman, that's highly unlikely."

As the summer waned, so did my optimism.

I was seeing a new therapist, David, on the urging of my friend Rosemary. Rosemary was the most extreme character among my friends. She was a fifty-year-old Jewish South African woman who'd been a cult, avant-garde film star in the seventies. Back then, she'd been happily entrenched in the experimental theater and film scene that featured hard drugs and orgies and from which some famous actors and musicians emerged. Rosemary herself was a wild and colossal spirit who was now sober. David was the therapist who had helped her get clean when she was using heroin and drinking vodka like water. "If David could wrangle me, he can handle you, Jessica." I could not argue with this logic. Like Mark Epstein, David was a practicing Buddhist, but he was also a cancer survivor.

David listened to my forecasts of doom. I felt as if my life and opportunities for happiness would be over on September 12. I'd had chance after chance to find love and now my time was up. "You are casting yourself in the role of the old maid, Jessica," David said. "This is not reality. This is a story you're constructing." I spent full days in bed. Dr. Smith started calling me at home every night to check on me. She wanted to know what my plans were for the next day and insisted that I not spend my time alone. I was touched by her phone calls, yet some nights I didn't have the strength to face her and wouldn't answer the phone.

One hot summer night, I dragged myself out to a party downtown with Jonathan and Alexandra and ran into an old friend, Ali Marsh. Ali told me she'd read my Op-Ed piece and had been thinking of me. Her best friend from high school, Anna LoBianco, also had the BRCA-1 mutation and had recently undergone double mastectomy and reconstruction. Unfortunately, she'd discovered she had breast cancer before she found out about the gene. She went through months of chemotherapy and was now having radiation. Ali told me Anna was in remission and doing well and would be happy to get together with me to talk about the operation and show me her new breasts.

Anna and I met at a coffee shop near her apartment on the Upper West Side. I don't know what I'd been expecting—all I knew about Anna was that she'd gone to a fancy New York prep school with Ali and was a year younger than I.

Anna walked in the door—this formidable woman with a strong, sturdy, easy sense of self. She'd lost her hair from chemo and her scalp was just beginning to show new growth, but she exuded health. An onlooker would have more likely assumed she'd shaved her head as a fashion statement. Anna apologized for being late—she told me she'd just ridden her bike across the park from her radiation appointment. I was awestruck.

Anna's spirit was so large that the moment I met her I felt my own energy recharge. Her eyes were remarkable. They were tawny-colored and through them you felt her power, humor, and warmth. This was not someone who'd be knocked down easily, by cancer or anything else. I had an image of her as Superman and the cancer as bullets bouncing off her chest. Anna told me she worked at the Bank Street College of Education uptown on 112th Street. I was not surprised to learn that she also sometimes taught a self-defense class for girls after school. Anna lived with her boyfriend, Chiq, and they had two kids—Ruby was almost five, and Dario was nineteen months.

Being around Anna for just five minutes shamed me. Here was a woman who had faced cancer, chemotherapy, radiation, and mastectomy all while working and raising two small kids. And she rode her bike across town to medical treatments! I was healthy, yet hiding under the covers because of an impending elective procedure. I felt embarrassed about making a fuss over breast surgery in light of all Anna had been through.

"The mastectomy was easy," Anna said, her eyes smiling. "It's cancer that was a bitch."

There was cancer all over Anna's family. Her maternal grandmother, Miriam, got breast cancer at forty-two and died of a recurrence at fifty-two. Miriam's sister Estelle had breast and ovarian cancer but beat them both and lived to be ninety-four. Estelle tested positive for the BRCA-1 mutation in 2002, and her daughter, Anne, tested negative. However, a year later, in her early sixties, Anne got breast cancer anyway. Miriam's brother, Lovey, did not get cancer, but his son, Martin, died of prostate cancer. Martin's daughter Kate was diagnosed with breast cancer in her forties. Lovey's daughter Laura was diagnosed with breast cancer and beat it. Laura's daughter, Fran, died of breast cancer in her thirties.

In spite of all this, neither Anna nor her sisters felt particularly alarmed over their own health because their mother, Dora, was in her sixties and had never been diagnosed with cancer.

In August 2004, a year earlier, Anna felt a small lump in her left breast while breast-feeding Dario. She assumed it was a swollen milk duct and paid no attention to it. A few weeks later, her milk wasn't producing properly, so she decided to stop breast-feeding. The lump did not go away.

Anna went for a checkup with her gynecologist in November 2004. Her doctor felt the lump and said it was probably nothing, but did a needle biopsy to be sure. The results were inconclusive. Anna scheduled an appointment with a breast surgeon.

In the next two weeks, Anna's tumor grew very big, very fast. It had corners and edges—irregular contours—and they were visible through her skin. She went to see the breast surgeon in mid-November. Another core biopsy was inconclusive, yet the doctor believed it was papillary breast cancer, a very treatable form. Since Thanksgiving was coming up, a lumpectomy was put off until the beginning of December. In the meantime, Anna took the BRCA test.

By the time Anna went in for her lumpectomy, she had learned she was BRCA-1 positive. The surgeon removed the tumor, but the BRCA results meant her chances of recurrence of cancer in the second breast were very high, so Anna would also need to undergo a double mastectomy. Since Christmas was approaching, the surgeon suggested they wait until after the holidays and scheduled Anna's mastectomy for mid-January. Strangely, he did not remove or check any of Anna's lymph nodes during the lumpectomy; apparently he intended to check them during the more extensive procedure. The tumor was removed and the doctor staged Anna's cancer at IIB. Anna and her family were relieved.

Almost immediately after the tumor was removed, another lump appeared under Anna's left arm. She called the surgeon's office. A nurse told her this was normal—it was drainage from the lumpectomy, not to worry. Christmas rolled around and the lump grew dramatically bigger. Anna called the office, was told that the surgeon was out of town until after the holidays, but not to worry. "Never get sick during Christmas," Anna advised.

At her January surgery, Anna's surgeon expressed alarm at the new, large lump. It was, in fact, a malignant tumor. During the mastectomy, the surgeon removed all of the lymph nodes from Anna's left arm and the sentinel node from her right arm. The cancer had spread to one lymph node. It was not good to have any node involvement, but one didn't sound terrible. After all, it could easily have spread to four, five, or six. However, Anna's cancer was "triple negative" for estrogen receptor, progesterone receptor, and HER-2/neu, which meant the cancer was aggressive.

Anna had the same reconstruction process I had chosen—expanders and silicone implants. She'd had the expanders put in during the initial mastectomy operation but had undergone chemotherapy before having her second exchange surgery. She was all put back together except for her nipples. She told me she wasn't that happy with the reconstruction because she'd wanted to have smaller breasts and her male plastic surgeon had bullied her into going bigger. It was hard to imagine someone bullying Anna, though I told her I'd had a similar experience with a male plastic surgeon in Los Angeles.

Despite her ordeal, Anna was amazingly calm and upbeat. She said the chemo had made her sick, but she'd never missed a day of work. When she started losing her hair, she just decided to shave it all off. She didn't bother to wear a wig or scarves. Anna said the idea of having cancer made her worry a bit about her kids, but mainly she was tough and in full remission—she'd just had a clear PET scan—and wasn't terribly concerned about it.

She mentioned in passing that a month after starting chemo, the doctor had discovered "some lymph node involvement in her chest"—an enlarged node beneath her sternum. She'd had some back pain, so they did a bone scan and something lit up on one of her ribs, which the doctor dismissed as a false positive. However, they found the sternal node on the bone scan. She said the node couldn't be removed, though they were treating it with radiation. She didn't make much of this, but it sounded frightening to me. From my experience with my mother, I knew too well that any stray cancer cells were bad.

Anna wanted to talk about my decision to have a prophylactic mastectomy. Her mother and her sister Yummy had just taken the BRCA test, and both of them were found positive. (Her mom was one of the lucky few whose mutation had never caused cancer.) Her second sister, Nina, had not yet taken the test. Anna was adamant that Yummy have a preventive mastectomy, and Nina, too, if she tested positive. Yummy refused to discuss it. Anna had forwarded my article to both her sisters and wanted to enlist my help in persuading them. I told her I would of course speak to either of them, anytime.

I walked with Anna to her apartment so that I could have a proper viewing of her newly reconstructed breasts. She lived in a one-bedroom with Chiq and their two kids, which made for cramped quarters, but the apartment had a wonderful, homey vibe. Ruby and Dario's artwork hung all over the walls, and everywhere were lots of photos of the kids, friends, and loved ones.

Anna took off her shirt in the bedroom and showed me her breasts. They were large—a C- or D-cup, but Anna was tall and big-boned and I thought they really suited her. There was a long, horizontal mastectomy scar across the middle of each breast, and no nipples. Anna said she hadn't yet gotten around to the nipple reconstruction, and didn't know if she would bother. Chiq didn't care and she felt fine as they were. What annoyed her was that they were so far apart. She tried to push them together to form cleavage and showed me how they wouldn't move. We both laughed about the new fake-breasts travails. This was the first time I'd seen her act girlish and it was very sweet. I told her I'd read about this cleavage issue online—the implants fit under the chest muscles and if your anatomy was such that the muscles were spread apart, there was no way to squish them closer together. But I thought her breasts looked great. I thanked her for meeting me, sharing her story, and flashing for me. We said we'd keep in touch on all matters.

I was inspired by Anna. She pulled me out of victim mode.

DANIELLE AND BRUCE were worried about me. They still believed that my decision was rash. Danielle felt that I was wildly underestimating how traumatized I would be when I woke up without my breasts. As he'd consistently done for my mother, Bruce wanted to do something special for me before my surgery. He came up with the most staggering gift—sending me and Danielle on an extravagant vacation to St. Barths at the end of August.

I could not believe my eyes when we got to the villa. It was all dark wood and billowing white curtains with rooms that opened onto a lush pool area and the turquoise sea beyond. This villa was fit for the honeymoon of a European princess, but it was mine and Danielle's for ten days. It would be the most indulgent vacation of my life—nothing to do but swim, do yoga, and, in my case, emotionally prepare for the loss of my breasts. This was the most peaceful oasis I could ever have conjured—an extraordinary present, impeccably timed—as my surgery was in two weeks and panic was beginning to set in.

St. Barths is a French Island and French women often go topless on the beach. For the first and only time in my life, I walked and swam and spent all day with nothing covering my breasts—in the privacy of our villa and in public by the sea. It was liberating, incredible, and—I felt—appropriate, all things considered.

It was rare for me and Danielle to spend so much time together. We shopped at the grocery store and cooked all our meals; we talked a lot about our mom. Danielle told me that she and Bruce were thinking about having a baby—nothing would have made our mother happier. I spent hours writing in my journal. I told myself that the choice I had made was claiming life, health, and future. It was an investment for my unborn children that I would be well, that I would be alive to care for them. I gave myself pep talks to act on my convictions without fear. And if panic set in when I woke up without my breasts, I would have antidotes to remind me why I'd chosen this path. I wrote: *Having surgery is taking care of my self. My true self. My spirit, my character, stuff on the inside. Whatever the cosmetic result of my body, my breasts, is not all that consequential.*

I built up my strength and courage during the day, but at night my subconscious took over. I dreamed that my teeth were falling out. I dreamed I was speeding in a car and there were no brakes. I dreamed that I was in New York City in a postapocalyptic world, running through the bombed-out streets, seeking shelter. But during my waking hours, I didn't feel anxious. I was identifying with the powerful reasons I had chosen my course of action.

While we were in the fairy world of St. Barths, Hurricane Katrina hit New Orleans. Danielle and I watched the devastation on television from so far away—horrible and surreal. Suddenly it occurred to me that I had considered scheduling my mastectomy at NOLA in New Orleans this week! It was an eerie near miss.

The last morning of our vacation, I sat on the floor of my bedroom in front of a large mirror and gazed at my naked breasts for an hour. It sounds ridiculous, but I felt sad for them. They needed to be sacrificed in exchange for my health. It seemed so strange that my own body could be a danger. That my own body could kill me. It was unfathomable. I stared at my boobs and assessed them critically. They were two large, sagging appendages. Then I considered them from another point of view. They were feminine, womanly, sexy. Natural, earthy, and beautiful. I felt remorse that I'd taken them for granted and complained about them all these years. Sitting there in the mirror was my own weird, private ritual of honoring them and saying good-bye. I thought about my mother. I thought about her breasts, which had been very similar to mine. I thought about how she'd always dressed to enhance them, how proud she'd been of "keeping her figure" through the years. Then I pictured her suffering and dying. I remembered her piercing eyes in those last weeks. *Never forget me, Jessica.*

I had no doubt that I was doing the right thing.

By the time I returned to New York, I was ready. In those final days before the surgery I was in a feverish, almost elated state. I knew I would have lots of visitors after the operation and I was preparing the apartment like a salon. I ran around the city searching for a rug—bought one and lugged it uptown on the subway; unrolled it, hated it, lugged it back down on the subway. Tried another one and did the same exact thing. This time my friend Rosemary had to accompany me because I was in such a tizzy. We got on an express train that took us deep into Brooklyn by accident—we ran up and down the stairs on the platform to switch trains, lugging the stupid rug like madwomen. As a present, my father went to the flower district and, with Danielle's help, bought seven large trees for Harriette's apartment—three for indoors and four to be lined up on the terrace. It was a tremendous gift, and symbolic—the trees breathed new, flourishing life into the place.

My friend Gillian, a photographer, insisted I would always regret it if I didn't document my breasts before the operation. I went over to her apartment one night and she spent thirty minutes setting up soft light to create beauty shots. Gillian and I had been friends since the ninth grade. I remember at fourteen writing the initials of the boys we'd kissed in the back of our math books (a grand tally of four between us). The night she lost her virginity she'd left her boyfriend's apartment in haste to come over and tell me every last detail of the most important event in our young lives. We'd laughed and cried and gorged on brownies on the living room floor. This night, with her two-year-old daughter asleep in the next room, we downed vodka tonics and laughed and cried together once again. The photo shoot with Gillian was intimate and emotional—the focus was on letting my guard down, allowing her to memorialize the beauty of my body in its natural state.

Several days later I had a photo shoot with Rosemary and Kay of an entirely different nature. We had a cheap digital camera that none of us knew how to use and a six-dollar bottle of wine. This experience was about freedom and defiance. Taped to my wall was a quote from *The Tibetan Book of Living and Dying*: "What is our life but a dance of transient forms?" I would revel that night in my present state of being—celebrating it in preparation for letting it go. Rosemary and Kay took their shirts off in solidarity (though Kay declined to be photographed). We ran around my apartment with abandon, put on Russian hats with earflaps, lay down on the table with roses strewn around us, struck poses like a topless Thelma and Louise using rose stems instead of guns.

My friends rallied around me—spoiling and celebrating me as if it were my wedding. It turned out to be one of the most joyful times of my life. I had a "farewell breasts" night out with a group of my closest girlfriends. Liza (Cokie Roberts's daughter-in-law) was eight months pregnant, but she ordered her husband to take charge of their two small children so she could spend the final weekend before the surgery with me. Calista and my agent, Jeff, flew in from California to be there for the operation. Jolie (who had taken care of our mother when she was ill) had worked as a nanny for Gillian all summer and was moving in to help Danielle take care of me for two weeks before returning to Poland. The day before the surgery, I popped into Limitone Salon to get my hair blown dry by Amir and startled everyone by cheerily telling them I would be removing my breasts the next morning. They gaped at me like I'd lost my mind, and were flabbergasted when I agreed to flash for Amir and Alon, two gay Israeli hairdressers.

This is something I would *never* have done before, but now I had detached from my breasts. I didn't see them as mine anymore; they were about to be gone, so showing them felt impersonal. "Oh my God!" Alon exclaimed. "I had no idea your tits were so *big*!"

Later that afternoon I went to Dr. Choi's office to have my breasts photographed using new 3-D imaging technology. This digital scanner would enable Dr. Choi to determine the volume and contour of the breasts. She had explained to me that these measurements were most useful in the case of single mastectomy, when they were trying to re-create a second breast to match the first. However, she was now taking 3-D scans of all of her patients to have detailed before-and-after records.

I took my shirt off and a young woman drew Magic Marker markings on my breasts. I didn't know if she was a doctor or a nurse or a medical student, but she was definitely younger than I. She told me she was going to take photographs from all different angles. Blue masking tape on the floor indicated where I would stand. As she drew on me, I asked, "Don't you think this is odd?"

"What's odd?"

"That my breasts are here. We're drawing on them, photographing them. And tomorrow they'll be gone."

She looked up at me as a young woman, a peer, rather than as a medical practitioner.

"It is odd. I can't imagine." Her eyes flickered with compassion. "I'm sorry."

The 3-D scan was a big box on a tripod, like an old-fashioned camera. I aligned my toes with the strips of blue tape, standing at a 90-degree angle, then at 45 degrees, then 0, as she snapped away. Then we did it all again on the other side. It was a somber experience, like last rites.

Suddenly, it was the night before the surgery. For "the last supper" I went to a restaurant with Jonathan, Alexandra, Calista and her son, Liam, and Danielle. Liam was about to turn five. Calista had told him they were coming to visit me in New York because I had to go into the hospital for a few days. He had drawn me a very detailed and colorful picture of a turtle on the plane to make me feel better. I'd always loved turtles (which Liam did not know) because I identified with the tortoise in the fable about the tortoise and the hare. I'd always been the last of my friends to hit significant milestones: In high school I'd been the last to have a boyfriend. In college I'd been the last of my group to lose my virginity. I'd been the last to find my footing in a career. Now I was the last to get married, and on my way to being the last to have a child. To me, the end of the race was arriving at a rich and fulfilled life. I always agonized over being so far behind, while I kept crawling along in my own slowpoke way, at my steady pace. Finally, finally, long after everyone had ceased keeping track of my progress, I would sneak up on them and cross the finish line with aplomb. I hung Liam's turtle on my hospital room wall. It remains one of my prized possessions.

NINETEEN

September 2005

anielle slept over the night before the surgery. We shared the queen-size bed, just as I had shared a bed with my mother all those months. I lay awake all night, staring at the ceiling and at the clock. Jolie slept on the sofa in the living room. Danielle and Jolie planned to live with me and take care of me for two weeks post-op.

Though sleepless, I felt remarkably calm. I was ready for battle. Strong in my resolve. I thought of what I was about to endure as a rite of passage into adulthood. Though I was thirty-five, I saw myself as much younger. If I hadn't felt like a grown-up before, I certainly did now. I'd taken my health and my future into my own hands. I, alone, had made this decision. No doctor had told me I had to do it. No one but I was responsible for this.

At five a.m., it was time to leave for the hospital. I turned to Danielle. "Okay, now I'm starting to get scared."

I sat in the admitting room with Danielle and my dad. I was

wearing a hospital gown and holding a gauzy blue hospital cap. Dani and I had looked through the gowns and chosen one with the small ("more feminine") pattern that our mom had preferred.

There was no escaping the familiarity of this scene. The three of us had been in this hospital, in an admitting room, presurgery, too many times before. I put on the little hospital booties. Once again, I was in my mother's shoes. With one enormous distinction: I wasn't sick. Thank God I wasn't sick.

I had put on a little blush and lipstick that morning while dressing for the hospital. I was, after all, my mother's daughter. I thought of her packed in the Hummer with me, Dad, Dani, the driver, and two dogs, en route to surgery, showing me her pink and lavender silk nighties: "I like to be pretty till the last minute!"

Danielle and I went into a presurgery changing cubicle to wait for Dr. Choi. She was going to come in and draw markings on my breasts, sketch out where the incisions would be made. Dr. Roses came by first. He gave us a warm greeting and introduced us to his chief resident, Dr. Kutchin, who would be assisting him. Dr. Kutchin was young and handsome. Dani gave me a look—*maybe I would end up marrying my surgeon after all!* Dr. Roses spoke about how our mother had been his patient and what a wonderful woman she was while Dr. Kutchin listened thoughtfully. Dr. Roses said he'd see me in the operating room and walked off. Before trailing him, Dr. Kutchin smiled at me and flashed two surgical hats—one red, one blue.

"You decide which color I should wear, Jessica. For luck."

I caught his eye. "Definitely the blue."

He tied the blue one on his head. "See you soon."

"He's flirting with you!" Dani said with excitement.

"You think . . . ? Thank goodness I put on blush this morning!"

Dr. Choi came in. I opened my hospital gown and she drew

lines on my breasts. Danielle sat beside me. The moment was surreal. My breasts were here, my body was whole. When I woke
up, they would be gone.

A nurse led me into the OR and I climbed up onto the operating table. The room was too bright. I felt like I was in a play. The
anesthesiologist asked me questions about writing for television
while putting the IV in my arm. Everyone perked up when I said
my friend David Zabel was the head writer on ER. I asked if they
watched the show, but before I heard the answer, I blacked out.

I have no memory of the first several hours after surgery. Danielle tells me I woke up in the recovery room happy and smiling
and pretty, too. "You're the only person who could come out of
five hours of surgery with her blush and lipstick looking fresh and
rosy!" Dr. Choi had placed tissue expanders under my pectoral
muscles and filled them with saline. Though I was bandaged and
had drains attached to me, you could see subtle breast mounds—I
was the tiniest size A. I had a morphine drip, was drugged and
loopy. Danielle said I was sitting up tall and showing off my new
"ballerina body."

The first post-op memory I have was from early that same evening. My dad had gone home, Danielle was out getting food, and
I was alone in a private room with a nurse named Verona. It was
like I had suddenly come to. I was aware of my surroundings and
I felt my body. My chest felt like I'd been run over by a truck.
I gasped from the pain, and Verona told me to press the button
for morphine. My bladder was painfully full. She helped me get
out of the bed and walk with my IV pole to the bathroom. I sat
there for fifteen minutes, ran water in the sink, but could not pee.
My stomach muscles were clenched and I could not relax them. I
started to panic. Verona went to get a nurse on the floor to put

in a catheter. Back in the bed, a nurse tried to insert a catheter but was having trouble.

"Relax!" she hollered. "You're too tense!" This launched a full-blown anxiety attack.

"Are you kidding? If I could relax I wouldn't need a goddamn catheter!" I yelled back. The nurse gave up on the catheter and gave me an Ativan instead. After an hour of sitting in the bathroom, listening to running water in the sink and shower, and putting hot, soaking towels on my forehead, I finally felt my muscles unclench enough to allow me to pee. Afterward, Verona took me for a walk around the floor. She put her arm around my waist. This maternal gesture made me realize I was yearning for my mother. In that instant, I remembered that my mother was gone, and my breasts were gone. We walked. I shook and wept.

I remained in the hospital for four days. They were a blur. My friends sent endless bouquets of flowers. I was too woozy to take phone calls, but Danielle told me who sent each arrangement. I allowed very few visitors.

Once home from the hospital, I had two large drainage tubes attached to me, one on each side. Clear tubing collected blood-tinged fluid from each of my breast wounds and connected to plastic containers that I wore pinned to my cotton nighties. The drains needed to be emptied and the fluid measured twice a day. I was high on Vicodin and felt no pain, so rather than recuperating quietly and prone, I hostessed an around-the-clock party for a week in my glamorous attire of nightie-and-drains. I hate to say it was like sitting shivah—thankfully this occasion was about life, not death—but shivah is the closest comparison I can make. Friends stopped by every day to visit, eat, and keep me company. Danielle was sleeping in the bed with me and Jolie was sleeping on the sofa;

my dad was always there. Jonathan, Alexandra, and Gordon came over every day. Kay, Gillian, and my friend Cara were constant presences. Cara had gone through a terrible break-up that week. She was traumatized, so she moved in with us and slept on the air mattress in my bedroom. My dad's old black Lab, Sam, had just been released from the animal hospital—his belly was shaved from surgery, he had a red cast on his leg, and he could barely walk. So Sam moved into the living room and slept on his dog bed. One afternoon, my friend Michael Panes came over and played the piano and we gathered around and sang show tunes. It was a circus.

The breast expanders were hard—like breastplates of armor. The drugs masked the acute pain, but my chest still ached. The expanders beneath the muscles applied a constant pressure. Many women on FORCE liken the feeling to an elephant sitting on your chest. I wasn't allowed to shower for over a week. Sleep—and shower—deprived, I was nevertheless a happy hostess. Like the week prior to my surgery, the first postoperation days were unexpectedly joyful.

Not surprisingly, Doctor Choi was less than pleased when she examined me in her office the following week. I'd been instructed not to raise my arms, engage in much upper-body movement, or lift anything. Instead I'd been running around the house, serving guests, making beds, and singing show tunes. I'd overdone it. Fluid had accumulated and was leaking out of my breast wounds. Infection after mastectomy and reconstruction can present complications. A generalized infection would have to be treated with either oral or IV antibiotics. If bacteria got around the implant and the infection didn't respond to antibiotics, it could become a serious problem. I did not yet have an infection, but I'd come close. Dr. Choi took out my drains and shut down the party.

Two weeks after surgery, Dr. Choi told me it was time to stop taking the Vicodin. A half day without drugs was a rude awakening. I'd had no idea my body was in such *pain*. Suddenly, Vicodin became the most precious thing in the world. I told Dr. Choi I was not ready to stop taking it. She wrote another prescription and I weaned myself off of it, slowly.

Two weeks after surgery, I went in to see Dr. Roses for an exam. He held the pathology report in his hand.

"You had precancerous changes in your right breast tissue, Jessica. Atypical ductal hyperplasia."

I was shocked.

"If you had any doubt about the course of action you chose, this should dispel it. You did the right thing."

TWENTY

October–December 2005

was in a hurry to be put back together again. The expansion process had to be completed before the next operation—the exchange surgery—could be scheduled. In that next phase, Dr. Choi would remove the expanders and replace them with silicone implants. I would then have reconstructed, natural-feeling breasts with no nipples. Three months after that, when the incisions healed, Dr. Choi would perform the third and final surgery—nipple reconstruction. The whole process would take five months from first surgery to last.

The faster I finished expanding my chest muscles, the sooner I could have the second operation. I saw Dr. Choi in her office every Tuesday for weekly fills. She'd inject a needle into each expander and add saline, gradually expanding the chest muscles to make room for the implants. Luckily, I'd chosen to create small new breasts, which meant I would not need to expand the muscles far, so the process would move quickly.

Each week I had the curious experience of walking around with a different breast size. After a lifetime spent at 32D, wearing a little black dress as a 32A was a novelty. I felt like Audrey Hepburn. But an A-cup seemed *too* small to keep. The next week I was a small B. I tried on an array of clothes to see how that felt. I was Goldilocks and the boobs were the porridge: "These are too small, these are too big, these are *just right*." But it didn't go in that order. After my Tuesday fills I would spend the remainder of the week trying out the new size. I was happy at 240 cc (a full B-cup) but I wasn't positive—maybe one size up would feel good, too. It didn't. After the next fill I felt large and busty in T-shirts again—that old feeling of self-consciousness returned. 240 cc was just right.

I did not experience pain during the fills, just a mild sensation of pressure, because I'd chosen implants that were 240 cc of silicone. Implants can be up to 700 or 800 cc. I read threads on FORCE in which women wrote that their muscle pain kicked in during the final fills—when the muscles were stretched to capacity. Because my new breasts were so small, I avoided this sensation.

Just over a week after surgery (once the drains were removed) I went out with Cara and Gillian to a cocktail party. I wore my Audrey Hepburn little black dress, heels, and red lipstick. No one would have guessed I'd just undergone a mastectomy or that my body was under construction. I was woozy from Vicodin, but to all appearances I could have been tipsy from Stoli or champagne. One or two acquaintances commented that I'd lost weight (my smaller breasts created this illusion). I felt self-conscious only when I hugged someone hello. My breasts were hard, like armor—surely anyone who hugged me would notice? No one seemed to. In the course of conversation I told a woman that I was a little out of it because I was on Vicodin as a result of surgery I'd had the previous week. "What type of surgery?" she asked.

"I have the breast cancer gene," I said. "I had my breasts removed." She was dumbstruck.

Whenever I would tell anyone in the weeks to come that I'd just had a preventive mastectomy, the response was always the same—disbelief. I don't know if it's because I looked young or because I didn't have cancer. It was probably a combination of both.

On November 7, 2005, about seven weeks after the mastectomy, Danielle escorted me to the hospital for the exchange surgery. The morning of my first operation I'd felt strong, fresh from ten days of swimming and yoga. This time, I felt weak and run-down before we started. My father was in Florida, so it was just me and Dani. We rolled out of bed at dawn and grabbed a cab to the hospital. I certainly hadn't bothered with makeup. We were sitting in a changing cubicle waiting for Dr. Choi when Dr. Kutchin, the handsome chief resident, showed up. I pulled the blue mesh hospital hat off my head.

"Hey, I'm doing surgery with Dr. Roses this morning and Dr. Choi told me you were here. I thought I'd stop by and say hello."

"That's so nice of you," I stuttered.

"So, how are you doing?"

"Good. You know . . . happy to put this second operation behind me."

"Well, good luck. I'll try to check in on you in recovery."

Dr. Kutchin left, and Dani and I turned into giggling, frazzled eighth graders.

"Did you bring my makeup? I need some blush!" I cried.

"Yes—it's in the bag. He likes you!"

"I look like hell—he said he was going to visit in recovery!"

"Don't worry." Dani took out a makeup brush and dusted my cheeks until they were rosy. "All better."

Dr. Choi arrived.

"How are you doing this morning?"

Dani flew into yenta mode.

"Dr. Kutchin just came by to see Jessica. . . . We were wondering if he's single. . . ."

"I think he is," Dr. Choi said conspiratorially, like she was one of our girlfriends. "I'll find out."

"The guy assisted in removing my breasts!" I said. "This is too bizarre."

"It's a postmodern world," Danielle replied.

I woke up in recovery feeling horrible. I was nauseous and my mouth felt like sandpaper. Through my haze I saw Danielle. Next to her was not Dr. Kutchin, but a nice, suburban Jewish mother.

"I'm Donna's mom," she said. "I ran all around the hospital trying to find you. Donna wanted to come, but she's in the admitting room. She sends her love."

"Send her mine," I said with slurred cotton-mouth.

As it happened, Donna's mastectomy was scheduled on the very same day as my exchange surgery.

"I'll call the hospital tomorrow to check on her," I said.

Danielle and I did not wait around to see if Dr. Kutchin showed up. We both felt ill and wanted to get out of the hospital and home to bed as swiftly as possible. As soon as we got to the apartment, I threw up. Once I vacated the bathroom, Danielle went in and threw up. I was sick from anesthesia; Danielle was newly pregnant. We were sick as dogs, in an apartment with one bathroom. Though we did find the humor in it, it was not a pretty scene.

Once again, I was bandaged and could not shower for a week, but at least this time there were no drains. And once again I was on Vicodin. My new silicone breasts felt soft and real to the touch, though they were completely numb. It was as if the doctors had shot Novocaine into both breast mounds. I was told that some patients regained feeling in time while some did not. The wounds were taped and I tried not to look at them. When I peeked, I saw a long, horizontal knife line across each breast. The incisions were stitched and scary-looking. There were no nipples.

Though the second operation was minor compared to the first, for me it was a more difficult recovery. The first operation was a symbolic triumph—I'd taken a brave step and all my friends and family had gathered around in support. This time, the procedure was sheer drudgery. I'd had a bad reaction to the anesthesia. It was just me and Dani vying for the toilet. When the nausea subsided, I got a bad cold. Everything felt darkened by a gray cloud.

About three weeks later, my wounds had begun to heal. I was off the Vicodin and allowed to drink. It was the night before Thanksgiving. I got dressed up and went to a party with Cara thrown by a woman named Nadia. We'd all been in a theater company together in the early nineties, and Nadia had been throwing this annual bash ever since. It was a homecoming of sorts for us to see all our old cronies. It was also an occasion on which everyone famously regressed, got drunk, hooked up, and pretended we were still twenty.

In the spirit of the night, I downed a few vodka tonics. I'm a lightweight drinker, so I was gone at drink number two. A handsome movie studio executive I used to date was there. My memory of the evening is blurry, but somehow I wound up in his arms with him telling me I was beautiful. He kissed me and asked if I wanted to leave with him. In that moment, I truly experienced a postmodern quandary. I'd just elected to remove my breasts in an attempt to preempt cancer and was only half reconstructed, yet I was in the arms of an attractive ex-flame. What to do? I left with him and insisted we go to the Waverly Diner, where I informed him of my travails over a milk shake and fries. He listened patiently, said all the right things—the mastectomy didn't matter, I was still appealing, et cetera. He was in town from Hollywood for a few days and said he wanted to see me over the weekend. He dropped me off in a taxi, kissed me good night, said we'd speak tomorrow. Not surprisingly, I did not hear from him again.

MY FAMILY was in Florida for Christmas. My dad was now spending winters in Del Ray, and Danielle and Bruce were planning their January wedding in Palm Beach. I usually love the Christmas season in New York. This year I could not get out of bed. The farthest I traveled was to my desk to halfheartedly type away at a book proposal about my BRCA experiences. In truth, I was in the thick of it and had no clarity, no perspective, and no clue about how to tell the story. I was still living it. I didn't know how it would all turn out, and that month, things were not looking up.

I spent a lot of time thinking about my mother, trying to wrap my head around the fact that she was gone. It had been over two years since her death, but the permanence of her absence still hit me in waves. She was such a vibrant human being. Where did she go? What happens to all that energy, striving, passion, yearning? It just evaporates? I also spent time thinking about Adrian. Previously, every time he had come into my mind, I'd pushed him away. I'd been grieving over so many other things, thinking of Adrian had just been too much. Now I remembered him, how alive I had felt in his presence. I Googled him and found a video of him performing stand-up in the eighties. I listened to his voice and watched his younger self with morbid fascination. I was dwelling on death and obsessing about my dead, married ex-boyfriend. I was not in a good way.

Once again, Jonathan and Alexandra came to my rescue, dragging me out of the house. I joined them at a Christmas party at a friend's apartment in the East Village. It was cozy and warm with Christmas lights twinkling on the small tree. I ran into Ali Marsh.

"How's Anna?" I asked. "I e-mailed her twice recently, but she didn't write back."

Ali looked tense.

"I didn't want to tell you this, because I didn't want to upset you, but she's not doing well. The cancer is back."

I gasped. It had only been four months since we'd met for coffee and she'd been in full remission.

"They found a lump in her remaining breast tissue?" I asked in horror.

"It's spread. The cancer is in her bones—her neck, ribs, and spine."

I burst into tears and so did Ali. We hugged and wept on the corner of a sofa while everyone else drank eggnog.

It was only much later that I would learn the details of Anna's illness. In mid-November she had been experiencing back pain and went for another PET scan. This time spots lit up in her mediastinum, cervical spine, left seventh rib, and right upper back. A bone biopsy of her rib confirmed that it was cancer.

Cancer in bones grows from the inside. It grows outward and ultimately breaks the bone.

One morning in late November, a mere ten days after she'd learned her cancer had metastasized, Anna sat up in bed, heard a snap, and felt piercing, indescribable pain. Chiq called an ambulance. Her neck had cracked. The CAT scan would show she had "a fractured cervical spine, but stable." She would wear a permanent neck brace.

Anna's mother was undergoing a hysterectomy that day at a hospital across town, and Anna's sister was with her, so Chiq called Ali to meet them at the hospital. Typically, Anna was the heartiest woman you would ever meet. She went through brutal chemotherapy treatment without uttering a complaint. Cancer had never fazed her. This day, in the hospital waiting room, in gut-wrenching pain, was the one and only time Ali ever saw Anna break down. Anna wept and cried, "I know the cancer's in my neck and it's so close to my brain—it's going to go to my brain! It's eating me alive."

TWENTY-ONE

January 2006

On New Year's Eve I had dinner with Rosemary at a Vietnamese restaurant on the Upper West Side, after which I walked her to the annual Alcoholics Anonymous New Year's Dance. We lingered outside for a while as she tried to persuade me to come in, but I refused. She ran into the strobe-lit church to find her boyfriend, Herb, at around eleven p.m., while I headed downtown toward Harriette's apartment on Fifty-seventh Street. I walked along Central Park South and as I neared Sixth Avenue, there were police barriers and masses of people. My street was blocked off. I fought through the crowd, trying to explain to the bull-headed officers that I *lived* on that street. After forty minutes, I finally dissolved into tears. I was now thirty-six, body under construction, alone on New Year's Eve, and stuck in a throng of intoxicated, shouting people wearing gold cardboard crowns and blowing noisemakers. "I should have stayed with the sober drunks," I thought. A young cop saw me crying and made his way over.

"Are you all right, miss?" he said. His kindness made me blubber all the more. I pointed to the awning of my building, uttered that I lived there. He escorted me across the street. I rang in the New Year in the elevator.

ON JANUARY 8, Danielle and Bruce were getting married. Danielle was three months pregnant and glowing. I was thrilled for her and happy to welcome Bruce as a brother-in-law. That said, the event was challenging for me.

My younger sister was getting married for the second time. She had never been particularly passionate about having children (as I was), yet she was now happily pregnant. I was the old-maid older sister, single and dateless, once again, at a pivotal family occasion. But what felt most overwhelming to me was the venue and tenor of the event.

The wedding was to be at Mar-a-Lago, the 110,000-square-foot estate in Palm Beach that had been built in the 1920s by Marjorie Merriweather Post and is currently owned by Donald Trump. The Spanish/Venetian/Portuguese-style manor sits on twenty acres of perfectly landscaped lawns nestled between the Atlantic Ocean and Lake Worth; *mar a lago* means "sea to lake" in Latin. Three boatloads of Dorian stone had been brought over from Genoa, Italy, to construct the exterior walls and arches. The estate has 58 bedrooms, 33 bathrooms, 12 fireplaces, and 3 bomb shelters. In addition to the Gold and White ballroom, Trump built a new, gargantuan 20,000-square-foot Donald J. Trump Grand Ballroom in Louis XIV style, with gold and crystal finish.

This over-the-top setting was not my style. It was to be a society wedding—Bruce's family was friends with many prominent, wealthy Jewish couples who summered in the Hamptons and wintered in Palm Beach. When I was fifteen, I'd announced to my parents that none of their friends would be invited to my wedding. Back then, I imagined getting married in a wheat field with all my artistic friends participating—singing songs or reading poems. At thirty-six, I thought that if I ever married, I'd probably elope. To this Danielle replied, "Your husband and his parents might have feelings on the matter. We're doing it for the family."

Another thing Danielle and Bruce did in honor of family was to request that guests donate to the Stephanie Queller Fund at the Lynn Cohen Foundation for Ovarian Cancer Research in lieu of wedding gifts.

Our mother would have been in hog heaven presiding over this lavish wedding (especially with Bruce as her son-in-law!), but she was not here, so I was the default hostess. Celebrating Dani and Bruce was the easy part. Putting on my game face and making charming conversation with the guests required every ounce of my energy. At Dani's first wedding, ten years earlier, all the ladies had sympathetically patted me on the back and said, "Your turn will come. . . . How old are you?" Back then I'd been twenty-six and had a boyfriend on my arm. Now it was pure farce. I was not just the older, single sister. Because I'd written the *New York Times* article, everyone present knew I was the mastectomy girl. As I made my way through the Donald J. Trump Grand Ballroom during the reception, the fancy Jewish ladies peered at me as if I'd just returned from Auschwitz. No one knew quite what to say to me. At least my new body really did suit me; the smaller breast size was flattering and clothes finally fit well. Many ladies exclaimed with surprise, "You're the sister? But you look so good!" Others clucked sympathetically. "Someday you'll have a fairy-tale wedding just like this one. Someday you'll find your Bruce."

By the end of the weekend I felt like a deflated balloon.

. . .

LATE IN THE MONTH, Donna and I made a date to go to a BRCA support group Dr. Smith had put together at the NYU Cancer Center. Before entering the room, we embraced and checked out each other's new bodies. Just as we'd planned, we had switched breasts—she was now a full C-cup and I was a modest B. Donna still had her expanders in; her exchange surgery was scheduled for the following week. My final surgery was two weeks away.

There were about a dozen women assembled in a conference room, most of them around our age. There was one genetic counselor presiding. Several of the women had just learned their BRCA status and were trying to figure out what to do. Several others had known their status for a while and had already undergone oophorectomy but were grappling over breast surgery. Donna and I were the only women present to have prophylactically removed our breasts. One young woman, age twenty-five, had breast cancer. She'd had a double mastectomy and was about to start chemo.

We went around the room. Each person recited her medical history and story. Afterward, we asked one another questions. I listened closely as women talked about having had their ovaries removed. There was debate about whether it was best to remove the uterus in addition to the ovaries. This alleviates the possibility of uterine cancer, but it is controversial because removal of the uterus may disrupt the structure of the pelvic floor. They spoke about early menopause, hot flashes, and vaginal dryness. There was discussion I couldn't really follow about whether to take hormone replacement therapy drugs. Because I was intent upon having children before removing my ovaries, I'd spent the past year and a half focusing solely on the breast issue. I had all of this to look forward to.

The young woman with breast cancer was astonishing. Her attitude was so positive and cheery, she could have replaced Kelly Ripa as Regis's cohost. She was doing a breast cancer walk in two weeks; she had all of her surgeries and procedures organized and planned out. Once again, I was humbled. I knew I would not have such energy or grace under those conditions.

Everyone in the room was curious to hear from Donna and me about our preventive mastectomies, why we decided to opt for them, and how our experiences had been. I said the surgeries had been pretty easy, all things considered. I was extremely happy with my new body in clothes. It was too soon to tell how the scars would heal, but I felt normal and natural and whole. I was worried about my personal life, but I felt quite at home with my new breasts. And it was a true pleasure never to have to worry about bras again!

Donna's contentedness was several notches higher than mine. She felt great. She *loved* her new breasts. And she still had the expanders in, which meant they were hard as rocks—she could only imagine how happy she would be with the soft silicone implants. She'd had sex with an ex-boyfriend the other day while half-reconstructed, with the expanders and no nipples. It had been great. He thought her new breasts were objectively sexy—the look and the roundness and the form. It hadn't been an intimate experience with someone who loved her unconditionally—it had been a sexual experience. He was genuinely turned on by her new breasts, which meant so much to her. She'd been afraid that her body would be defective and unsexy. She no longer had those fears.

I was quite envious, listening to Donna speak. I'd not yet had an intimate experience with a man and I still harbored those very fears.

Most important, Donna and I both expressed our relief to no longer have the threat of breast cancer looming.

At the end of the meeting, Donna and I took our shirts off for the room. I had to laugh. I'd bared my breasts for others so many times since this BRCA issue had taken hold of my life (just like Suzy and Anna had). I, who had always been shy about walking around topless in front of boyfriends, was suddenly whipping my shirt off with the casual nonchalance of a pro. Donna and I allowed the women to touch them. Everyone ooh-ed and ahh-ed over how pretty our new, nippleless breasts were.

In the weeks before my final surgery, I remained in a state of low-grade depression. I was ashamed of this—I knew I'd done the right thing by having the operations and wished I felt confident and empowered—but I didn't. I was filled with sorrow. I was consumed by my nonexistent personal life. All I wanted was a family—a partner and children. I was afraid that those things would pass me by. I was acutely aware of my accelerated biological clock because of the necessity to remove my ovaries at forty.

My best friends kicked into gear. They were going to fix me up on dates the moment I recovered from the final surgery. Gillian was the most forceful yenta and cheerleader. I was touched by her efforts but had no faith that they would amount to anything. I reluctantly agreed to go out on blind dates, with the caveat that she had to inform the guys of my situation in advance. If the breast cancer gene and mastectomy freaked them out, best to know up front. I had no desire to break the news to them over dinner. Gillian agreed and put out feelers.

Danielle slept over the night before my last operation. Dr. Choi had said I should choose the nipple size I wanted, so Dani and I traced paper circles using quarters and a NyQuil bottle cap, cut them out, and held them up to my boobs. Dani designed and selected the right size. She is a great sister.

The next morning, we waited for Dr. Choi in the admitting room changing cubicle. A few weeks earlier, my friend David Zabel, the head writer of *ER,* had asked me to write a freelance episode and I'd mentioned this to Dr. Choi. I'd asked her if she had any good medical stories to share with me. We'd agreed to go out for drinks when I'd recovered from the final operation so she could tell me her war stories. When Dr. Choi met us in the cubicle, she reported that she'd mentioned my *ER* episode to Dr. Kutchin and had arranged for the three of us to go out for drinks! We'd orchestrate via e-mail when I was feeling better. Even my plastic surgeon was setting me up on dates. . . .

I opened my hospital gown and held the paper circles Dani had designed up to my breasts; Dr. Choi agreed they were the right size, and she traced them with Magic Marker. She also marked my hips; I had opted for skin grafting in reconstructing the areolas rather than just tattooing in color on the advice of my sister's ob-gyn. As it happened, Danielle's doctor had undergone a prophy-lactic mastectomy herself after her own mother died from breast cancer. I had accompanied Danielle to an appointment, and the doctor had showed me her reconstructed breasts, which looked fabulous. She'd done skin grafts and insisted it was the only way to go. It gave the reconstructed nipples texture, made them look uncannily real. After they healed, you could tattoo in color. We were taking the skin from both hips; the scars would be hidden beneath the panty line.

I put on my booties and blue mesh hat, kissed Dani good-bye, and once more walked into the operating room.

• • •

I LAY IN BED bandaged like a mummy. I was again swathed across my chest where my newly grafted nipples were stitched and raw. I had long, diagonal stretches of gauze and tape along each hip, and my left forearm was elevated in a soft brace. (Dr. Choi specialized in both breast and hand surgery, so I'd asked her to remove a harmless cyst from my left wrist while I was already sedated in the operating room.) Since I had no feeling in my breasts, I felt no pain from the stitched nipples, but the wounds along my hips and on my wrist hurt.

While I was bedridden and bandaged, phone calls from men started to pour in. My friend Meredith had asked her husband's aunt, a doctor, to set me up with some eligible young surgeons. Gillian had wrangled two men for me who lived in Los Angeles: both were divorced with young children. One was a screenwriter, one was a sportswriter; both were said to be attractive, though one of them was allegedly quite short.

I listened with detachment to the messages they left. I couldn't keep track of who was who—I'd call Meredith or Gillian and ask, "Is Andrew the doctor or the screenwriter, and is he the short one. . . . ?" If these guys only could see the woman they were calling. I looked like the sit-com version of a person who'd been in a car wreck, with arms in casts and a leg in traction. My friends had informed these potential suitors that I'd undergone a prophylactic mastectomy; they hadn't mentioned I'd had the final operation *yesterday*.

I called back a couple of the guys, made stilted small talk, and said I was "busy" for the next week or so.

Four days after my surgery, I got a call from Mark, the sportswriter.

Mark was forty-three, recently divorced, with a six-year-old daughter. He'd grown up in Manhattan in what he called the "projects for white people" in the West Twenties. He'd gone to Stuyvesant High School (my dad's alma mater) and then Swarthmore, got his graduate degree at Columbia University's journalism school, and had been a reporter for twenty years. He'd covered murders, drug dealers, and corruption under the tutelage of Pete Hamill (his "rabbi") at the *New York Post* and *Daily News* in addition to being a sports columnist at both papers for over a decade. In the past few years, he'd become an acclaimed sports biographer.

Mark was an old-school character, cut from the Hemingway/ Mailer cloth—a hard-drinking, tough-talking writer who was also a boxer. In that first conversation, my heart melted at the paradox of this intense, stomping-bull alpha male who talked so tenderly about his young daughter. He had joint custody and was Mr. Mom 3.5 days a week. "Every morning at six a.m., my daughter says, 'Daddy, I'm hungry!' so I get up and make her French toast. I'm a master at girls' hair—I blow-dry, do braids, barrettes, ribbons. And I can tell you about every princess—Ariel, Belle, Jasmine, whatever."

Mark was a New Yorker to the core but had been living in Los Angeles for about nine months. His ex-wife had urged him to sell their Brooklyn apartment and move the family out to California. As soon as they got there, she left him. He was furious and tried to take the divorce proceedings back to New York, but soon discovered he would risk losing his daughter, so he had no recourse but to make peace with LA. To say the least, Mark was a fish out of water in Hollywood. He'd hardly left the six-block radius of his house and office since he'd arrived; he had no clue how to pronounce the names of major boulevards like La Cienega and Cahuenga.

Mark and I talked on the phone for over an hour. I was smitten. I'd found him charming and funny and full of heart. I told him about the book proposal I was writing and about my decision to undergo prophylactic surgery. He responded with admiration for my choice and bravery.

The next day, Mark called again and left a message on my machine: "I was thinking about your book, and I have a few ideas. . . ." I called him back, and he really *had* been thinking about the book. "Breasts are the only organs in the body that are both maternal and sexual," he said. "I think there's a lot to mine out of that." We talked for over two hours. I still had my apartment in Los Angeles and said I'd be out there in two weeks.

The next day, Mark left another message on my machine. "So, I have some more thoughts about your book. . . ."

I called him back. "You don't need to use the book as an excuse to call me, you know," I said. Again we talked for two hours. And then for two more hours later that night. Mark and I talked on the phone for four hours a day for the next two weeks.

During those weeks, I was floating. I could scarcely eat or sleep. My depression was a faint, distant memory. I was now over the moon. I hadn't even met this guy, but I was already in love. He'd written a best-selling biography of Joe Namath. I'd gone to the bookstore and bought several copies, but they only had the paperback edition in stock, which did not have an author's photo. I would talk to Mark on the phone and gaze at the photo of gorgeous Joe Namath, conflating the two of them in my mind.

I canceled dates with the other guys, though I did go out for drinks with Dr. Choi and Dr. Kutchin. They told me wacky medical stories to inspire my freelance episode of *ER*. We had a good time, but Dr. Kutchin no longer held appeal. My heart was taken.

I arrived at the Burbank airport late one night in March, around eleven p.m. Since Mark and I had never met, we'd decided to go out on a proper date the following evening. But I called him when I landed and we both realized we couldn't wait another day, so he drove across town to my apartment at midnight and was waiting for me on the steps when my cab pulled up. He was carrying champagne, caviar, and vodka. He was incredibly handsome, over six feet tall, with an athlete's body to match his tough-guy persona. As it turned out, Mark had Namath's coloring and beautiful hazel eyes. We had as much chemistry in person as we did over the phone.

From that moment on, every night that Mark did not have his daughter, we spent together. I flew back to New York for a few days to pack up all my things and officially moved back to Los Angeles. I didn't end up writing the *ER* episode, because I took a full-time job on a new show instead. My body was still healing, so I mainly wore camisoles when we were in bed. Mark made me feel beautiful, sexy, and whole. He often said he did not mourn the loss of my natural (and large) breasts—he loved the modest size I chose. He was a man who'd always been with gorgeous women and cared about such things—yet he insisted I was the most beautiful woman he had ever known. He loved me all the more for the courage to do what I'd done. "You're not only beautiful, you've got balls," he would say with admiration. Mark swept in and erased all of my fears.

A few weeks later, I met Mark's daughter and fell madly in love with her. Mark's hazel eyes shone out of this dazzling creature—all limbs and long, light brown hair. She was six but had a husky little Demi Moore voice and her daddy's intensity and humor. She'd make fun of him, doing a perfect imitation of his New York accent and tough-guy vernacular: "Yo, yo, yo, we're the Bo Brothers, from the old neighborhood! You better watch out, or I'll knock you out!"

Mark's daughter warmed to me instantly. She was affectionate and always in my arms. My heart would soar when people mistook her for my daughter. Soon enough, the three of us had become our own little family unit. I was living the domestic life I'd been craving. And I knew Mark wanted at least one more child. I felt blessed.

IN MID-JUNE, I met Anna LoBianco's sister Nina for breakfast in Hollywood. She brought her baby boy along. Nina had finally taken the BRCA test and discovered she was BRCA-1-positive, just like her sisters, Yummy and Anna. Neither Yummy nor Nina had been planning to undergo prophylactic mastectomy, but Anna had been imploring them to do so. Recently, Nina found a lump in her breast. She told me she was getting a needle biopsy in two weeks. She was freaked out and wanted to talk to me about my elective mastectomies.

I asked Nina how Anna was doing. I'd gotten periodic updates from Ali and I'd sent Anna e-mails over the months but she hadn't replied for a long time. Nina said the cancer had continued to spread—just as Anna had feared—and had reached her brain. Anna had been wearing a neck brace since Christmas and now used a walker to get around. Still, Anna was doing astonishingly well. She continued to go to work every day. A few weeks earlier, on her birthday, she'd had a big party at Bank Street College, where she worked. Anna had been a vibrant hostess. Nina's partner, Jodi, used to be in a lesbian punk band called Team Dresch. A few days after Anna's birthday, the band reunited at the Knitting Factory for a benefit for Anna, to raise money for her medical bills. Anna sat in the wings backstage, singing along to every song and rocking out. At some point, Anna got up onstage to give the drummer a handkerchief to wipe off her face. As Anna slowly walked onstage wearing her neck brace, she pretended she was going to dive into the audience as they screamed and applauded her. She laughed and returned to her seat. The following night Anna insisted on going to Brooklyn to see Team Dresch perform again. Anna had been ecstatic both nights. Her body was failing, but her energy was vital and clear.

Nina and I talked about my choice to undergo the surgeries. I told her that by far the *fear* had been the worst part. I was afraid I'd feel deformed, afraid I wouldn't feel at home in my reconstructed body, afraid that my sexual partners would find me unappealing. Afraid that somehow the physical and emotional consequences of my choice would sabotage my ability to find love. None of this turned out to be the case.

The surgeries themselves—while not pleasant—had been relatively easy. A few months later, I had my full range of motion back and felt 100 percent fine. There was simply no comparison between the inconvenience of surgery and the horror of fighting cancer.

We talked about the statistics. A woman who is BRCA-1-positive has up to an 87 percent chance of developing breast cancer. Nina told me that her oncologist had declared—based on her family history—that Nina was certainly at the top of that scale; she had an 87 to 90 percent chance of contracting the disease. I'd been told that now—postmastectomy—I had a 1 to 3 percent chance. As I mentioned, the average American woman has a 10 percent chance of developing the disease. I was elated by my new odds.

Nina asked about my feelings regarding oophorectomy. I told her I planned to do it at around age forty, because I wanted to have children first. She said she'd like to have a second child and would definitely remove her ovaries afterward.

We went to the bathroom together and I took my shirt off and showed her my breasts. We remarked how Anna had shown me *her* new breasts just under a year ago. Nina was amazed at how real my reconstructed nipples looked—I told her that skin grafting was the secret. My scars were still quite prominent, but that didn't faze her. Nina decided she was going to do it.

TWO WEEKS LATER, Nina got a call from her mother and Yummy saying that Anna was very ill. The cancer was now in Anna's lungs; her breathing had grown shallow and she could barely speak. Nina and her partner, Jodi, shoved some clothes in a suitcase, grabbed their son, rushed to the airport, and got on the next flight to New York. When they landed, Nina had a slew of messages from Yummy on her cell phone, increasing in their urgency. Nina left Jodi to deal with the baggage and their child and jumped into a taxi. She called Yummy and sat helplessly on the other end of the line as she listened to Yummy and her mother weeping and soothing Anna: "Just think of beautiful things, Anna. Just let go."

"I'm trying. . . ."

Anna LoBianco died just after midnight on June 29, 2006. Nina heard her sister die over the phone as she rushed to the hospital in a taxi. Anna had just turned thirty-six.

TWENTY-TWO

July 2006

anielle gave birth to a healthy, gorgeous baby boy on July 11. Miles lit up our lives. Dad was thrilled to be a grandpa. Pictures of his grandson hung all over his house and were copied onto mugs. He bought bibs and clothes and stuffed animals. He went to the mall in Florida and ordered a dozen children's CDs with Miles's name added to the songs.

Danielle flourished as a mother. Every milestone filled her with joy: the first time Miles pulled himself up in his crib; the first time he ate baby food; the first time he started babbling consonant sounds. Danielle said the greatest feeling she'd ever experienced was when she went into the baby's room each morning and he lifted up his head, recognized his mommy, and broke into a smile.

I, of course, thought my nephew was brilliant (and still do). At six months, Miles had games he played with me and entirely different ones with Danielle. I'd plunk him down on my bed and say, "Good night, Miles," and he'd bury his face in the pillow and pretend to be asleep, then pop up. I'd say, "Miles is awake!" and he'd break into giggles. We had a cuckoo clock game in which he tilted his head back and forth to the sound of my saying "tick-tock." Miles could sit before a mountain of toys and he would always reach for the books. He'd make sure the book was right-side-up and proceed to turn every single page, studying the pictures and letters with intensity until he got to the end, and then he'd reach for the next one.

Mark and his daughter spent time in Southampton with me, my dad, Danielle, Bruce, and Miles. Mark was wonderful with the baby. His intense, domineering personality transformed into an almost maternal quiet while holding Miles.

After I'd finished my final surgery and while Danielle was still pregnant, she told me she had changed her mind, she *would* take the BRCA test, after all. Going through the surgeries with me had made her realize mastectomy and reconstruction were not nearly as terrifying as they sounded. I had recovered quickly, with little psychological trauma, and my cosmetic results were great. Dani said she would take the test after she had the baby.

But she did not mention the BRCA test after Miles was born. Occasionally, I would bring up the subject, ask if she'd given it any more thought, but she would deflect the question. What I did not know is that she had privately taken the test when Miles was about two months old. She told no one—not me, not her husband, not our father.

She had tested positive.

Like me, she had been stunned. Somehow because we each had a fifty-fifty chance of inheriting the gene and I had tested positive, Danielle thought she would test negative. No such luck. For several months she kept this secret. Though rationally she knew having the mastectomy was the right thing to do, she wasn't emotionally ready to check herself into the hospital and begin the process. And she didn't want to be pressured to do so.

Eventually, Danielle told Bruce. Just one year earlier, when I had been preparing for my operation, Bruce thought I was nuts. He changed his mind once I got the pathology report back and was informed that I'd already had precancerous changes in one breast. Bruce had been on the front lines as our mother battled ovarian cancer. He urged Danielle to have the surgery.

Several weeks later, Dani told me her results, and soon after she told Dad. Now that she had a baby, Dani felt an enormous responsibility to remain healthy. She would have the mastectomy, she just didn't know when. Maybe she would have another baby first.

IN FEBRUARY 2007, Danielle, Miles, and I moved into our mother's Southampton house. It had been three and a half years since she died. For most of that time, we'd rented the house to a lovely family. We had locked all our mother's personal effects into several walk-in closets and stored the rest in the enormous finished basement. Our tenants had recently moved out. After much discussion, we decided that the house was too expensive to keep and required too much maintenance to continue to rent. It was a heartbreaking decision, but we put the house up for sale. Now it was time for us to go through our mother's lifetime of belongings.

Our mom was a grand materialist and also a hoarder who'd amassed a tremendous amount of possessions. Her childhood of deprivation had made her perpetually afraid that she would run out of money and be unable to take care of herself, so she stashed emergency provisions. She never bought one of anything. Be it Saran Wrap or Frederic Fekkai shampoo, my mother had every-thing in dozens. The same principle applied to clothes, shoes, china, silver, bedding, towels, and everything else. For two weeks, we went through her stuff, day and night, sorting what to keep, what to send to storage, what to give to charity, and what to throw away. Every decision was emotional. "Do we keep Mom's slippers? What about her lingerie? Her T-shirts?"

One afternoon, while going through endless file cabinets in the basement, Danielle unearthed a huge red book, dated 1995, filled with our mother's handwriting. It was a day-by-day diary of her battle with breast cancer. Our mom was not a literary type—it was not in character for her to keep a diary, and it was shock-ing to us that she had. The entries began in January and ended in November. Danielle sat on the floor and read it from start to finish, tears streaming down her face. Then she handed it to me and I did the same. Neither of us remembered all that much about the horrors of our mother's breast cancer, because it had been eclipsed by the terrible ovarian cancer that had killed her. Here, in our mother's own hand and words, was a detailed account of her suffering. The shock and horror and fear when she was diagnosed, the devastation when the news kept getting worse—the cancer was stage II, it had spread to lymph nodes, she would require ag-gressive chemo, she would lose her hair. The nausea, fatigue, and chronic sore throats that resulted from treatment. The aching and tingling of her scalp as her hair began falling out in clumps. The sleepless nights of terror and weeping. The wigs, mouth sores, swelling of her arm from lymphedema. Having gotten through the first few chemo sessions and wondering how in the world she would ever survive months and months more.

Danielle felt that our mother was speaking directly to her from beyond the grave. She was telling her to have the operation and have it now, not to wait for cancer to strike.

Danielle scheduled her mastectomy date for March—four weeks after discovering the diary.

The night before her operation, Danielle and I talked on the phone every hour on the hour—two, three, four, five a.m. Neither of us slept a minute. She was scared. She didn't want to do it. She did *not* want to show up at the hospital and let them remove her breasts. Unlike me, she was very attached to her natural breasts. She didn't want to change them; she certainly didn't want to lose them. She'd cried hysterically for most of the day and had taken Ativan at night to calm her nerves. I begged her to postpone the surgery. I didn't think she was emotionally ready. She refused. She'd been having nightmares about getting cancer. "What happens if I wait until the fall and I get breast cancer over the summer? I will never forgive myself." Danielle was only thirty-three. I felt relatively confident that waiting six months would not harm her. Though she was terrified, she would not budge in her decision. "I'm going to walk through the fire."

I was filled with far more anguish over Danielle's mastectomy than my own. Our dad, Bruce, and I sat with Danielle in the admitting room; it was her turn to wear the hospital gown, cap, and booties. This time we were in Lenox Hill. Danielle had chosen her own surgeons at a new hospital. She had too many bad memories of our mother fighting for life at NYU. She wanted new energy.

Danielle's breast surgeon stopped by while we were in the admitting room. Dr. Lauren Cassel had been written up in many publications as one of the finest surgeons in New York. She was also the most glamorous doctor I had ever seen. She wore a short mink coat, jewels, and Manolos. "What a perfect doctor for Danielle," I thought. "Our mother would *love* her."

She was also compassionate. Tears were streaming down Dani's face (and mine) as Dr. Cassel soothed her. "You will be just fine. I promise."

Danielle's plastic surgeon was equally dazzling. Dr. Baraka was a distinguished, handsome man with a vague European accent, also impeccably dressed. Lenox Hill was truly an Upper East Side hospital.

When Danielle woke up in the recovery room, woozy from anesthesia, she wept. "I hope I did the right thing," she said.

Dani had a much more difficult recovery than I had, due to a preexisting autoimmune issue that was exacerbated by the surgery. She did not suffer much pain in the breast area, but was in tremendous pain systemically, triggered by the operation.

Her breasts healed beautifully, though, and Dr. Baraka did exquisite work. Dani had a hard physical recovery, but did not suffer emotional anguish over her breasts. She liked them right away. Like me, she adjusted quickly and easily. "The new breasts don't feel like that big of a deal," she said.

One other way in which Dani and I differed was on how we approached sharing our travails with other people. Danielle was fiercely private. She didn't want *anyone* to know she had tested positive or that she was having the surgery. She didn't want people to gossip about her or feel sorry for her. She'd decided to have the operation and tell people later, when she was reconstructed and the ordeal was behind her.

THE LYNN COHEN FOUNDATION for the prevention of women's cancers asked if they could honor me and Danielle with the Courageous Spirit Award at their April benefit. Danielle was extremely hesitant because the benefit would be held between her first and second operations. Her body would be under construction and she didn't know whether she'd be ready to "come out" by then. On my urging, Danielle agreed. The event would take place (fittingly) at Fred's, the posh restaurant on the top floor of Barneys. Danielle's in-laws would be attending, as would her best friend from California, and her friend's mother and husband.

The day of the benefit, Danielle freaked out. She regretted saying she would do this; she didn't want to go, didn't want to give a speech. She wasn't ready to talk about this experience or make sense of it or articulate her feelings about Mom. She felt out of control and miserable.

I felt terrible, as I'd encouraged her to accept the award. I thought it would be meaningful for her to be admired and honored for her bravery. It was too late for her to cancel, but I told her I would deliver the speech for both of us. She wouldn't have to say a word.

As always, Danielle arrived at Fred's looking smashing. Not a soul would have guessed she'd been an emotional wreck a mere hour earlier. The crowd was young—they were our peers. Danielle and I were both dressed in black cocktail dresses and made up. We blended into the crowd. No one could have picked us out as the award recipients, as the women who'd just undergone mastectomies.

After dinner, near the end of the night, we were called to the podium. I had written a speech and read it aloud while Danielle stood by my side. When I was done, Dani took the microphone and to my great surprise delivered the most eloquent extemporaneous speech about her decision, our mother, and our relationship as sisters. When she finished, the whole room was in tears. Danielle looked like a blond supermodel. She had the beauty and élan that all the young Upper East Side women at this benefit aspired to. Danielle had stood up, with confidence and grace, and shared her decision to take the test and to take surgical action. She left everyone in the room in awe.

THOUGH MY BRCA status was an unhappy reminder of her own high risk of breast cancer, my friend (and Jonathan's wife) Alexandra participated in all the events surrounding my surgeries—the "farewell breasts" girls' night out, the last supper, the hospital days, the mad-tea-party soirees where I wore drainage tubes attached to my nightie. After I was put back together again, Alexandra told me I'd given her the courage to take the BRCA test—something she'd previously thought she would never do.

It is one thing to decide to take the test in theory—it's quite another to actually do it.

Alexandra had a baby boy, Sam, shortly after Danielle had Miles. Once she had a child, she, too, felt pressure to protect her health. Alex had been a young girl when she witnessed her mother die of cancer—she did *not* want her son to endure the same horror.

Yet Alex dreaded taking the test. Her mother was an Ashkenazi Jew and died of aggressive breast cancer in her early forties—all the signs pointed to the likelihood that she had carried the gene, which gave Alex a 50 percent chance of inheriting it. I'd tested positive and Danielle had tested positive, which made the possibility of receiving bad results all the more real.

Alexandra scheduled an appointment with Dr. Smith and took

the test—and discovered she was negative for both BRCA mutations. Though there's always a possibility of mutations that have not yet been identified, the biggest—and most likely—threat was removed. We were all elated. For the first time in her life, she was free of the burden of feeling that she was destined to inherit her mother's illness.

TWENTY-THREE

The creators of *Sex and the City* wrote and filmed three different endings for the series finale: In one, Carrie ends up with Barishnikov; in another, she ends up with Mr. Big; and in the third, she remains single—continuing her quest for love and identity. The reason they went to the trouble and expense of shooting three endings was to keep the *real* ending under wraps—it was a secret even from the actors and crew, so there was no chance of it leaking out. Rumor had it that the producers screened all three endings in front of test audiences to ascertain what the public wanted to see happen to their darling modern single woman Carrie Bradshaw.

Millions of women around the country watched with vicarious pleasure as Carrie got her fairy-tale ending—the unobtainable rogue prince Mr. Big gallops into Paris crying mea culpa and asks her to live with him happily ever after.

Others were disgruntled with the finale. Anyone who had invested years in following the travails of Carrie and Mr. Big knew that they'd never *really* just waltz off into the sunset. One of the reasons *Sex and the City* had struck such a chord with its audience was that it had managed to capture the complexities of modern dating life with an emotional veracity (even if glamorized by money and designer clothes). This Cinderella ending insulted a lot of loyal viewers. Mr. Big wouldn't reform his ways for long; Carrie would have too much self-respect to stay with a man unworthy of her—if the creators had remained true to these characters, the relationship would not work out. But test audiences proved suckers for the fairy tale.

In my life—in real life—there was no test audience.

After a year together, Mark and I broke up.

We'd met just as we were each emerging from traumatic situations. We clung to each other and promised ourselves to each other before we'd gotten the lay of the land. Mark healed me and made me feel beautiful, scars and all. The questions that had plagued me: What is a woman? What constitutes femininity? Would I be sexual, desirable without my natural breasts? Mark answered those for me. He made me feel not less of a woman, but more of a woman for choosing life. I believe that our relationship also restored him after the painful dissolution of his marriage. But it grew apparent that this relationship was not going to have a fairy-tale ending. Our personalities were too intense, and ultimately too combative, for a peaceful union. With mutual love and respect, we parted ways.

I am now thirty-seven, with the perilous threat of breast cancer behind me and the threat of ovarian cancer still looming. I will have my ovaries prophylactically removed at forty. I am ready to have a baby.

The questions I'd asked myself in a frenzy when I first discovered I carried the breast cancer gene—Could I no longer afford to be true to my beliefs about love? Would I have to marry the next man who'd have me in order to bear children?—I've since answered. No, I do not have to compromise my ideals. I will not choose a partner out of fear or the pressure of a biological clock. I've made bold choices throughout my life so that my external circumstances would reflect my internal convictions. I was born with a name that I found diminishing; I realized I had the power to change it. I inherited a gene that statistically ensured I would get cancer; I took action to prevent it. Love hasn't worked out according to my timetable? I will have a baby on my own and wait for love to unfold as it may. And so, dear reader, I'm heading to the sperm bank.

As I've already learned, the advances of biotechnology offer an array of choices, but they also come with ethical dilemmas. I've decided to purchase sperm and be artificially inseminated, but I can take it a step further. A technique called preimplantation genetic diagnosis, or PGD, would enable me to create embryos in Petri dishes and genetically test them for the BRCA mutation. I could then choose to implant only the embryos that do not carry the mutation.

I believe in utilizing biotechnology to promote health. Of course I don't want my children to inherit the breast cancer gene, but there is no existing method to alter the genetics of an embryo. The only option is to select the embryos that do not carry the faulty gene. Had this technology been available in 1969, I would have ended up in the trash can. Can I, in good faith, choose embryos that don't have the mutation and destroy the others? Is taking action to ensure my unborn child will not have to go through the terrors my mother, sister, and I have suffered the responsible choice? Or is it immoral to extinguish a life merely because it carries a gene that I myself live with?

I'm about to dive into these uncharted waters.

Biotechnology is not just changing the lives of those of us who happen to carry a rare cancer mutation. Genetic tests are being woven into the fabric of modern life. The field of genetics is advancing at a remarkable pace, and these discoveries will soon affect every one of us.

Testing for birth defects has already become a routine part of prenatal care. The test that measures the level of alpha-fetoprotein (AFP) in the mother's blood during pregnancy may signal abnormalities such as Down syndrome, spina bifida, or other neural tube defects. AFP screening may be included as one part of a two-, three-, or four-part screening. Multiple marker screening is not diagnostic, which means it's not 100 percent accurate, but it determines who should be offered additional testing such as amniocentesis. These tests raise excruciating ethical questions of their own: Under what circumstance would a prospective parent choose to abort? Which diseases would be acceptable and which unacceptable? And what percentage of risk is the cutoff point? Do you abort if your unborn child has a 60 percent chance of a genetic disease? What about a 25 percent chance?

How far will we go in engineering embryos? I read about a case in London in which a couple has created embryos at a clinic that will screen them to make certain their baby will not be born with a squint. The father- and grandfather-to-be have severe squints that cause their eyes to look only downward or sideways. Embryos with the genetic mutation that causes this squinting condition will be discarded.

There are currently about twenty genetic tests available for different forms of hereditary cancer. On May 4, 2007, a front-page article in the *New York Times* announced a gene identified as a risk factor for heart disease. The genetic variant increases the risk of heart ills up to 60 percent and is so common that 50 percent of people in Europe are believed to carry one copy of it. On March 18, 2007, the *New York Times* presented a cover article about a twenty-three-year-old woman who opted to take a genetic test for Huntington's disease—an incurable, fatal brain disorder that renders its victims unable to walk, talk, think, or swallow. She tested positive. As of now, there is no treatment for Huntington's disease. People like this young woman seek the information so that they can be prepared for what lies ahead of them and make the most of the healthy years they have left. Many people are also seeking out the genetic test for Alzheimer's disease with the same rationale: Though there is no treatment or cure, they want the knowledge so that they can plan their futures accordingly.

In 2001, CNN covered a story about a couple in Atlanta, the Nashes, whose daughter, Molly, was born with multiple birth defects due to Fanconi anemia, a genetic disease that often leads to leukemia. Her best chance for survival was a perfectly matched stem cell transplant. The parents decided to create embryos and select one that did not carry the genetic variant for Fanconi anemia. This embryo became their son, Adam. Technology enabled the Nashes to give birth to a healthy child and to use Adam's umbilical cord blood for a transplant for his sister, Molly. It was the first time the PGD procedure had been used both to create a healthy life *and* to save an existing life.

These tests and technologies are not without their perils. They present complex, intensely personal dilemmas. But their value is incalculable.

ANNA LOBIANCO'S SISTERS, Nina and Yummy, decided to undergo prophylactic mastectomies a few months after Anna's death.

Nina chose not to get reconstructed. She decided she didn't want any surgeries other than what was medically necessary. "And living without breasts is a way for me never to forget Anna," Nina said, "to have her in my life, to be reminded of her every single day."

Anna asked that her ashes be scattered at a river in Portland, Oregon, that she loved. Nina, Chiq, and several of Anna's friends made the trip to fulfill Anna's wishes in March 2007, nine months after her death.

"We went to the river on a rainy, gray day," Nina said. "The ashes were in a plastic bag. There was so much of it. As we scattered Anna's ashes into the river, I thought: she's a part of everything, she's in the ecosystem, she's helping things to grow. This river meets the Pacific Ocean. Anna's everywhere."

It made me think about how, at the moment of my mother's death, I was staring out at the Atlantic Ocean. I was awed by the vastness of the sea. Through my grief, I felt the interconnectedness of all life.

My mother and Anna lived fervently until their lives were cut short. Their illnesses served as warning signs to us, their families. We are living in an age in which scientific advances give us new opportunities to *live*. Seize them.

Acknowledgments

The list of friends, family, doctors, and nurses who helped me, my sister, and my father through the events narrated in these pages is so vast it would require another book just to fit all of the names. Due to space, I must limit myself to acknowledging those who directly helped with the writing of this book. To the others, who generously embraced me and my family in times of crisis, I thank you from the bottom of my heart.

I'm indebted to Dr. Anne Moore, Dr. Robert Porges, Dr. Daniel Roses, and Dr. Franco Muggia for taking the time to answer questions about my mother's medical history. Also to Andrea Downey, my mother's oncological nurse, for sharing her poignant memories of my mother.

Profuse thanks to the lovely Dr. Miyhe Choi and her partner, Dr. Nolan Karp, for having drinks with me one evening and expounding on the subject of breast reconstruction. How can I ever thank the incomparable Dr. Julia Smith? One winter afternoon I spent four hours in her office grilling her on book-related topics, and still I had more questions. She insisted I come home with her, where she whipped up a gourmet dinner, cracked open a bottle of wine, and talked with me until one in the morning. Her knowledge and passion are rivaled only by her boundless generosity.

I owe an immeasurable debt to Dr. Steven Katz, who signed up to be the book's medical expert and adviser. Over endless cups of coffee, Dr. Katz explained all aspects of the BRCA gene to me in layman's terms. His patience was Herculean. The gifted Dr. Katz was on call for me around the clock, frequently e-mailing answers to my frantic questions in the middle of the night. Knowing that Dr. Katz was there to oversee the medical aspect of the book gave me tremendous peace of mind.

I could not have written this book without substantial help and support from Liza Roberts, Calista Flockhart, Erika Dilday, Scott, James, and Max Burkholder, Rosemary Hochschild, Jonathan Glatzer, Meredith Elson, Michele Juskowitz, Mark Epstein, Edith Gould, Molly McCarthy, Rob Mandel, Cynthia Morris, David Lubliner, Elise Henderson, Roberta Saft, Liza Wherry, Linda Larkin, Zandy Hartig, Fran, Leon, Michael, and Stacey Queller, John Norris, Joyce Wadler, Rick Kaplan, Kathleen McDonnell, Elsa Reich, the *Gossip Girl* writing staff and assistants, Alan, Michelle, and Tess Heilpern, and Matthew Kirshner.

Special thanks to Ron Schwary who gave me my first job and break as a writer. He gave many, many people their breaks in Hollywood. They don't make them like Ron.

I'm deeply grateful to Jennifer Westfeldt for her insightful, devoted help on the proposal, and to Rebecca Kirshner, whose prodigious talent was always available to me if I needed it. Also to Gordon Greenberg, who did everything from assembling the desk

I used to bringing over emergency provisions whenever I was too lost in writing to go to the store.

David Zabel, the mentor. He read the first sixty pages of the book and gave me notes before I dared show a word of it to any other person, just as he's been the first to read everything I've written from the start of my career. David is an extraordinary teacher and an even better friend. Words cannot express the depth of my gratitude.

I would not have made it through the writing of this book without Jonathan Marc Sherman, Kay Dilday, and Gillian Zoe Segal. Jonathan and Kay swept in as crisis managers whenever I got bogged down in a paragraph. One or the other would read the problem section with incisive eyes and offer a simple solution. I wrote the book at night during the fall and winter months of 2006 and 2007. Jonathan and Kay each kept me company via Internet or phone during writing breaks in the lonely hours when the rest of the world was asleep. Gillian handled all photography crises—touching up photos on a moment's notice for the S&G catalog or for publicity. She took over the morning shift of keeping me company on breaks when the sun had come up and I was still typing.

Cara Buono shared the burden of talking to me on the phone every few hours to keep my spirits up through the months of writing. Cara Buono and Kelly Wolf were the first people to read the manuscript from beginning to end. Their genuine, effusive responses soothed my fears, and made me feel that this was actually a book. Cara also took the author photo for the book jacket. I hate cameras. I am lit up with happiness in the photo because my eyes are reflecting my beautiful friend.

No one was more instrumental to my writing process than Jillian Bach. About halfway through the draft, Jillian offered to read each chapter as I wrote it and give me feedback before I turned it in to my editor. Jillian doggedly waited up at night for new installments and gave me the most thorough, frank, and thoughtful notes. She was my barometer of whether I had remained on-track or veered off into loopiness and self-indulgence. Jillian's devotion was incredible, and her honest responses gave me such comfort. I will be forever grateful.

Mark Kriegel, thank you. For buoying me during the process of pitching the book. For sending me to Julie Grau. Most important, for bringing me back to life.

I am profoundly indebted to the women who allowed me to chronicle their BRCA experiences. My deepest thanks to Alexandra Shiva, Donna Estreicher and family, and Suzy Hurley and family. In all humility, I thank Anna LoBianco's sisters for sharing such intimate, painful, powerful moments from Anna's life. I also thank Ali Marsh for sharing her private memories of Anna. I'm honored to portray Anna's magnificent soul in this book.

Many thanks to my superb William Morris agents: Andy Mc-Nichol, who sold the book with vigor, and Suzanne Gluck, whose support has been steadfast. Special thanks to the magnificent Cara Stein, who crossed departments to take the book on as a passion project. Cara is smart and formidable and warm all at once. I am so very grateful to have her in my corner.

Boundless gratitude to my manager, Jeff Wise. Our history is old-school: he took a chance on me when I had no professional experience, had faith in me when no one else did. Jeff passionately stood by me through all the personal turbulence that has interrupted my career. His unconditional support has been amazing. His friendship invaluable. Jeff has been my lighthouse through many dark storms.

I am so very proud to be among Spiegel & Grau's first books.

Spiegel & Grau is not only an elegant, first-rate imprint, it's an exceptionally warm, nurturing group. I'm profoundly grateful to Cindy Spiegel, Alison Rich, Kirk Reed, and Gretchen Koss. Above all, I'm grateful to my editor, the smashing Julie Grau. Julie is a force—a rare combination of tough-minded intelligence and humanity. Her passion for the book made the project feel special from the start. Her emotional support carried me through to the end. As a first-time author, I could not have felt more embraced or valued.

I am grateful to my brother-in-law for his abundant generosity. My mother loved him like a son, and I love him like a brother.

To my brave, brilliant, beautiful sister, Danielle Queller. Your tremendous support of the book means the world to me. Your unconditional support in all ways is a pillar in my life. I love you and don't know what I would do without you.

Lastly, to my father, Fred Queller. My lifetime champion and supporter. The most generous father in the world. I'm so happy to have the opportunity to thank you in print for believing in me always.

March 5, 2005

OP-ED CONTRIBUTOR

CANCER AND THE MAIDEN

By Jessica Queller

LOS ANGELES

Five months ago, I took a test for something called the BRCA genetic mutation, which is often referred to as the breast cancer gene. My mother had fought off breast cancer and she waged a ferocious battle against a second cancer, ovarian, when it ambushed her body seven years later. The cancer won.

After my mother's death, doctors and other cancer-savvy friends suggested that my sister and I should, at some point, be genetically tested for the faulty BRCA gene. I was 34 when I took it. I tested positive.

BRCA mutations are known to cause early-onset cancer, and statistics show that having the mutation means it's almost certain that I will develop breast cancer at some point in my life. It also means that I have a greatly increased chance of developing ovarian cancer. I share this gene with my mother, but I now have something my mother did not: the warning that, in all likelihood, cancer will be coming for me.

With tests like these, modern science acts as a crystal ball—warning us of dark events that may come. We seek such knowledge so we can take measures to protect against illness. Unfortunately the test for the BRCA gene is just a decade old, and doctors can offer no definitive guidance to women diagnosed with a genetic predisposition to cancer. In the case of BRCA mutations, science has outpaced our understanding of what to do with the data. Because the test is unaccompanied by any clear medical recommendations, it doesn't provide solace so much as open a Pandora's box.

My mother never took the test. In 1993, when she was 51, the test did not yet exist. As far as she knew, she was a paragon of health when doctors delivered the crushing news that the barely discernable spot on her mammogram was breast cancer and had already spread to five lymph nodes. She was a healthy, vibrant, beautiful woman who ran four miles along the Hudson River each morning before donning her Manolo Blahniks and catching the subway to her designer's showroom in the garment district. She didn't smoke or drink. She was slim and a careful eater. She hadn't the vaguest notion that she had a genetic predisposition to cancer.

My mother came of age in the early 1960's, and was a portrait of the "modern" woman. She had been raised by a single mother in a small house on the outskirts of Beverly Hills. With little but raw talent and determination my mother flew east to New York City, and by her mid-20's she was a successful clothing designer on Seventh Avenue. Along the way, she found an adoring husband (my father) and gave birth to two daughters. My mother was among the first generation of women that balanced family and career. She lived her life freely, choosing her spouse, her profession and the timing of her children according to the natural rhythms of her life. Then she was blindsided by cancer.

I see my life as the negative image of my mother's. I'm 35, accomplished in my profession, vital, healthy—yet weighed down by the burdensome information of my genetic legacy. It's akin to Eve taking a bite of the apple. Once you have the knowledge, there's no turning back.

Although I'm currently cancer-free, the knowledge of my genetic predisposition requires me to squarely face excruciating life choices—yet with inexact information. Breast cancer genetic screening is so new that doctors don't really know what to tell women with BRCA mutations except to be vigilant about increased surveillance. Preventative chemotherapy has proven effective for women who carry the BRCA2 mutation, but it does not work for carriers of the BRCA1 mutation (the one I have). The surest way to prevent breast and ovarian cancers is to have your breasts and ovaries removed. Recent studies show that undergoing these radical surgeries will reduce the risk of inherited breast and ovarian cancers by 90 percent.

However, I'm single, dating, and I want to have a family. I won't consider having my ovaries removed until after I've had children (thankfully the risk of ovarian cancer is slighter than that of breast cancer). But what about a double mastectomy? Having witnessed the death-grip of cancer, I'm not inclined to wait around for it to strike, especially since inexact surveillance machines do not always catch it at an early stage. Aside from drastically interrupting my life, how might a double mastectomy adversely affect issues of sexuality? My romantic future? How early in the dating process do I reveal the information about my faulty gene, with all its ramifications?

My sister is 31. She's not certain whether she will take the test. She remarked recently on the diametrically opposed approaches we have taken: knowing that cancer is often a genetic legacy, I sought out the knowledge that would permit me to make informed decisions. Knowing that there is a 50 percent chance she did not inherit the gene, my sister is not yet willing to give up the luxury that our mother had—to live her life freely, unaffected by the shadow of illness.

I empathize with my sister's point of view but in spite of the burden, I believe that women like me are fortunate to have the knowledge, imperfect as it is, of the likelihood of cancer—to know what our mothers did not.

I can say without question that my mother would have traded those 51 years of innocence for the dark knowledge that could have potentially saved her life. My mother would have done anything to live.

Resources

BE BRIGHT PINK
A Web site offering support and resources for young women who are at high risk for breast and ovarian cancer
P.O. Box 10915
Chicago, IL 60610
Lindsay Avner, Founder and Executive Director
E-mail: Lindsay@bebrightpink.org
http://bebrightpink.com/

FACING OUR RISK OF CANCER EMPOWERED
A comprehensive source of information on all BRCA issues
16057 Tampa Palms Blvd. W, PMB #373
Tampa, FL 33647
Phone: (954) 255-8732
Helpline: 866-824-RISK (7475)

E-mail: info@facingourrisk.org
http://www.facingourrisk.org/

NYU CLINICAL CANCER CENTER
The Center organizes support groups in the tri-state area solely for young women diagnosed with the BRCA gene
160 East 34th Street
New York, NY 10016
Psychosocial Support Group Focused on the Needs of Young Women: Lisa Sevanick, LCSW, 212-731-5110
http://ci.med.nyu.edu/

DR. JULIA SMITH
Director of Breast Cancer Screening and Prevention at NYU Cancer Institute. For those who live in the NYC area, Dr. Smith is the very first call to make. She's a brilliant and compassionate doctor who specializes in guiding high risk women through the complex issues surrounding the BRCA mutation.
212-831-0810

BREASTCANCER.ORG
A Web site featuring the latest breast cancer news and research
7 East Lancaster Avenue, 3rd Floor
Ardmore, PA 19003
http://www.breastcancer.org/

SUSAN G. KOMEN FOR THE CURE
A grassroots network of survivors and activists fighting to raise awareness and find a cure
5005 LBJ Freeway, Suite 250
Dallas, TX 75244

Phone: 1-877 GO KOMEN (1-877-465-6636)
http://cms.komen.org/komen/index.htm

THE BREAST CANCER RESEARCH FOUNDATION
A foundation that provides funding for innovative clinical and genetic research at medical centers worldwide
60 East 56th Street, 8th floor
New York, NY 10022
E-mail: bcrf@bcrfcure.org
http://www.bcrfcure.org/

THE BREAST RECONSTRUCTION GUIDEBOOK BY KATHY STELIGO
An informative manual offering practical advice on breast reconstruction
Carlo Press; 2nd edition (September 30, 2005)
http://www.carlopress.com/

1. Throughout the memoir, Jessica struggles to define her concept of beauty, an idea inherently influenced by her mother's uncompromising aesthetic and her grandmother's Hollywood glamour, even as Jessica tries to renounce those influences in her life and in her closet. Examine Jessica's evolving attitude toward beauty. How is it challenged and changed by witnessing her mother's death and by being diagnosed with the BRCA mutation?

2. Though Jessica and her sister, Danielle, share the experience of losing their mother to cancer and both testing positive for the BRCA gene mutation, they cope with their diagnosis in drastically different ways. Jessica chooses to go public—writing an Op-Ed piece, appearing on *Nightline*, and writing a book. Danielle chooses to handle her situation privately, telling as few people as possible. Compare these different ways of coping. Which is more in line with your own personality?

3. Following her operations, Jessica writes about being "made whole again" and "putting herself back together." Do you think she views her mastectomy and reconstruction in a circular sense or as a trajectory? Is this an act of rehabilitation (a return to her healthy self) or of transformation (an arrival at a new place in her life)?

4. Many people in the medical field are now labeling people who test positive for certain genetic mutations as "previvors," approaching them as if they are already sick. Do you think this label is prudent and helpful or extreme and unnecessary?

5. After receiving her BRCA positive status, Jessica enters a period of intense reflection and exhaustive questioning as she comes to terms with the decision she must make. Is there anything important that she *doesn't* consider? If so, what?

6. By taking the test for the BRCA gene mutation, Jessica embraces the "burden of knowledge" that science now affords us—the chance to know our genetic destiny. If you were in a similar situation, would you choose to find out what you could from science or would you forgo the opportunity and enjoy the freedom of not knowing what might be in store? How would you have advised Jessica if she had asked you whether she should get tested for the gene mutation?

7. Toward the end of the book, Jessica explains recent scientific breakthroughs in determining the genetic composition of embryos and, similarly, the newfound potential for parents to essentially pick and choose the traits of their child at the embryonic stage. What moral and ethical implications—both positive and negative—could arise from this practice?

8. Before Jessica's mastectomy, she tapes a Buddhist saying to her wall: "What is life but a dance in transient forms?" Aside from its literal application, what does this mantra mean in Jessica's life?

9. Of her first relationship after her reconstruction, Jessica writes, "Mark healed me and made me feel beautiful, scars and all. The questions that had plagued me: What is a woman? What constitutes femininity? . . . Mark answered those for me." Why did Jessica need to be in a healthy relationship to answer questions that she couldn't answer on her own? How do you think she defines womanhood and femininity at the end of the book?

10. Though Jessica relies on a small number of men, she is primarily buoyed by a fierce sisterhood of family, friends, and strangers bound together by a common disease. Examine the presence of sisterhood in this book and its powerful effect on Jessica's experience.

11. The act of bearing witness plays an important role in *Pretty Is What Changes*. Stephanie Queller kept a private journal of her fight against breast cancer, the women of FORCE congregate on the Web to recount their experiences in minute detail, and Jessica shares her story by writing a book. What motivates these women to articulate their experiences? Is it a means of coping? An act of power and defiance? An attempt to educate others? A way to leave a legacy?

12. How does Jessica broaden the notion of inheritance in her book? What does she inherit from her mother and how does she reconcile that inheritance—emotional, genetic, material—with her own designs for her life?